The First Complete Guide to Successful Tracking Training for Novice and Expert

Includes Training for Canadian Tracking Dog Excellent

First Printing – 1975
Fifth Edition – 2003 Revised
Sixth Printing – 2006

Published by
Barkleigh Productions, Inc.
970 West Trindle Road
Mechanicsburg PA 17055
(717) 691-3388 • Fax (717) 691-3381
E-mail: info@barkleigh.com
www.barkleigh.com
www.off-lead.com

Printed and Bound the United States of America
ISBN: 0-914124-04-8
Library of Congress Catalog Card No. 75-14693

Glen R. Johnson
1938 – 1991

The author was an Assistant Master at St. Clair College of Applied Arts and Technology in Windsor, Ontario, Canada. He was also the Training Director for Guardian Training Academy, a director of the Essex County Humane Society, President of the St. Clair Canine Associates, head trainer and team captain of the Guardian Angels Dog Demonstration Team and was the founder of the Windsor All Breed Training and Tracking Club, as well as being actively engaged in training dogs professionally.

In 1960, Mr. Johnson began training dogs in England with the British Alsatian Association. Here he became interested in, and familiar, with the many facets of security work and the training of sentry and police dogs, as done by the Royal Air Force and the British Police forces.

In Toronto, he initiated what is still considered the best demonstration team in Canada for the German Shepherd Dog Club of Canada and taught dogs to walk tightropes eight ft. above the ground while carrying a raw egg, setting a Canadian record for vertical wall scaling at 9 ft., 3-1/2 inches, etc. This was performed at the Canadian National Sportsman's Show for two years, as well as at the Metropolitan Toronto Police Games at Varsity Stadium. Over these two years, the team performed more than fifty times before the public. He was a past Director for the German Shepherd Dog Club of Canada and the founding Chairman for its Toronto Obedience Branch.

The author became fascinated with the tracking tests held at widely spaced intervals during these years where he could not get over the trouble trainers were having training their own dogs for this highly regarded title. He embarked upon a course of research, experimentation and documentation that enabled him to formulate his own training program that has resulted in 100% of all dogs completing the program earning a tracking title. Old wives tales went out the window and theories became irrelevant, as the program was based solely on "observable behavior" of those dogs that were already trained to track. The results of these experiments, and the program itself, are detailed in "Tracking Dog — Theory and Methods."

From this program, the youngest dog to ever acquire its TDX title in Canada earned his title at thirteen months of age. Before this time, there was never more than one dog with a TDX title alive anywhere else, and one student has two TDX dogs and a third with a Canadian and American TD. Only two other dogs have earned all nine training titles open to all breed competition in North America, and both of these dogs took their tracking training under Mr. Johnson's program. (At the writing of this book.)

The author believed that the only reason so few trainers acquire their tracking titles, or even attempt training for them, was the absence of comprehensive information on training methods that made training dogs for tracking simple and easy to follow. TRACKING DOG offers the reader this information.

Tracking Dog Theory & Methods

*I am dedicating this work to the two women
who made this book possible...
my wife, Sylvia, for all her help
and criticism during its creation,
and Ilene, the best handler
of tracking dogs I've known,
for her help in producing the manuscript.*

*If it weren't for the help
of these two ladies,
the information presented here
would still be
in the minds of a select few.*

Foreword

The late Glen Johnson was an Assistant Master at Saint
Clair College of Applied Arts and Technology in Windsor,
Ontario, Canada, but his passion was the dog's nose and all the
wondrous things it could do. He spent the last of his productive
years studying it and learning how to encourage it to work for
humanity. This book represents the fruits of his labors and is
considered the ultimate guide for those who wish to train dogs
to use their noses.

He based his program on the "observable behavior" of those
dogs that were trained to track and put those observations into
terms everyone could understand. He then developed a
comprehensive training schedule which, if followed, would lead
to tracking success. The results of these experiments and the
programs he developed are detailed in his manual *Tracking Dog
– Theory & Methods*.

Before his program there was never more than one dog with
a TDX title alive anywhere. After training with this program,
one student had two TDX dogs and a third with a Canadian and
American TD. Also, from this program, the then youngest dog
to ever acquire its TDX title in Canada earned his title at
thirteen months of age. Many dogs and their handlers have
attained their tracking titles using only this book for instruction.

Mr. Johnson's personal dog, *Avenger,* (the cover dog) was the first dog in history to not only earn its Canadian UDTX and American UDT but earned its SchH. Ill and FH degrees as well. At one point, only two other dogs had earned all nine training titles open to all breed competition in North America, and both of these dogs trained using Mr. Johnson's program.

It is the opinion of many tracking veterans that the sport is what it is today because of Glen Johnson's dedication, tireless energy, analytical nature, and special talent for teaching dogs and people. Glen Johnson opened the doors for the average dog handler to enjoy success at tracking.

Glen spent every waking moment proving the ability of the dog's nose and teaching others how to make it work for them. He showed us how to use dogs to track on a sidewalk, detect tiny leaks from natural gas pipelines, detect pollutants under the blacktop of the streets of New York City, detect gypsy moth egg masses in the wilderness, and many other tasks. It was he who foresaw *variable surface tracking* and made it a reality. All he ever needed to hear was "I wonder if..."

Thanks, Glen!

Don Arner
Past Publisher of *Off Lead* Magazine

Contents

Introduction to the Tracking Dog

Illustrations

Diagrams

Charts and Illustrations by Don Arner

Photographs

Photographs by Walter Gough

A, 3, 4, 10, 11, 12, 13, 14, 15, 16, 17, 18, 19, 20, 21,
22, 23, 24, 25, 26, 27, 28, 30, 31

Introduction to the Tracking Dog

Words cannot begin to describe the emotional thrill experienced by handlers at their first licensed tracking test when their dog's head lifts out of the grass with the leather article, signifying a tracking title well earned. The utter loneliness of being in trouble and the chilling pain of hearing the disqualifying whistle are feelings shared by all of the participating handlers, creating a unique camaraderie among the competitors that is not seen at any other competition involving dogs. This is the Tracking Test, final judgment of a man-dog team's ability to track in the eyes of Kennel Clubs around the world. No scores are given, no placements of first, second or third are made and dogs need only to preform satisfactorily once to earn their title.

This book has been designed to enable training enthusiasts to successfully train their dogs for these competitions and for advanced work that is required by efficient tracking teams. Before starting into the book, we should first have a general idea of what is expected of the dog and handler at these licensed tracking tests and what the titles actually mean.

In North America there are two tracking titles open to all breed competition. In Canada and the United States the first title is the Tracking Dog (T. D.), with very few differences in expected performance, and an advanced tracking title is licensed

---

in Canada that is called Tracking Dog Excellent (T. D. X.) and is passed by only the very best trackers.

Tracking Dog Test (T.D.)

In order to enter this test, the A.K.C. requires that a licensed tracking judge attest to the fact that a tracking team is in fact capable of passing a tracking test before the person can enter licensed competition. In Canada, the show giving organization may or may not require this procedure, as they deem fit. This procedure is called "certification."

The performance expected in both countries consists of the dog using its olfactory prowess to follow where a stranger has walked to locate an article he has dropped at the end of the trail. This stranger, or "track layer," as he is called, will leave a stake in the ground where he starts, so as to identify the beginning of the track and a second stake thirty yards along the track to show the handler what initial direction was taken. Continuing on, the track layer will execute several turns, two of which should approximate right angles, for a total distance of about 500 yards where he shall deposit an article that was previously approved by the judge or judges. The track will not cross any bodies of water, and no other conflicting tracks will be instituted.

The handler and the dog keep out of sight of the track while it is being laid, and will be instructed by the judge(s) when to start. This will be sometime after the track layer began, but not sooner than thirty minutes nor later than two hours. The handler shall start his dog between the first two stakes, and should the dog experience difficulty before reaching the second stake, he may be restarted once more. There is no time limit, provided the dog is working, but a dog that is off the track and is clearly not working should not be given any minimum time, just on the chance that it might pick up the track again. The handler may not be given any assistance by anyone.

In case of unforeseen circumstances, the judge(s) may, in rare cases, and at their own discretion, give a handler and his dog a second chance on a new track. A dog that is working too fast for the conditions may be restrained gently by the handler at the end of the lead, but any leading or guiding of the dog constitutes grounds for calling the handler off and marking the dog "failed."

The ideal performance by a dog should include his following the actual track closely in a steady, consistent manner, executing the turns precisely where the track layer turned, and never stop working until he identifies the location of the article. The manner in which the dog treats found articles shall be left to the discretion of the handler as to whether it is *retrieved* or simply *indicated*.

Tracking Dog Excellent (T.D.X.)

The dog is required to demonstrate its ability to track a stranger over varying terrain for a distance of at least 1,000 yards, crossing one road and crossed by two fresher tracks at widely spaced intervals. The track shall not be less than three hours old, shall contain more than five turns and have three articles deposited on it by the track layer. The first article will be placed at least 250 yards from the start, and the third article will be located at the end of the track.

The start of the track is marked with a single stake beside which the track layer shall trample down an area of one square yard, remain standing for one minute, then proceed to lay the track at a normal walking pace. The articles are to be dropped at irregular intervals directly on the track, and after dropping the third article, the track layer shall proceed for another 20 yards before turning to leave the area.

One hour after the track layer completed laying the track, a second stranger to the dog shall start from a point designated by the judge(s) and cross the original track in two places.

The articles deposited by the track layer must be articles that the track layer has had in his possession for some time in order that they have had time to become thoroughly permeated with his scent. They must not be larger than a pocket book or glove and not of a color that will contrast sharply with the background.

The dog must be given ample opportunity to take the scent at the starting point marked by a single flag. He should be so trained that he will slowly, and without coaxing from the

---

handler, explore the trampled starting point. No compulsion of any kind is to be permitted before the tracking commences, while setting the dog on the track, or during the tracking itself. If the handler has reason to believe that the dog has not taken the scent properly, he may re-start the dog once, provided that the dog has not proceeded more than five yards from the starting flag. Encouragement is permitted, but its unnecessary use is discouraged. When at a turn, the handler should stand still and allow his dog to circle until the dog indicates the direction of the track.

The handler will hold found articles in the air, momentarily, and retain them until the end of the track, after which they will be examined by the judge(s).

Should the dog discover and then follow the cross tracks for a distance of twenty-five yards, the dog is to be failed. The dog must find the last article and one of the other two in order to be marked "PASSED."

The licensed tracking test(s) found in most countries sets a performance standard by which tracking teams, consisting of a handler and dog, may be evaluated. Many excellent trained tracking teams never enter tracking competitions, such as working police tracking dogs, the military and other official agencies. For the average dog-training enthusiast, these standards of excellence give the opportunity to test the ability of his training in tracking and provide him with opportunity to stand with his head high and proudly state he has a trained "Tracking Dog."

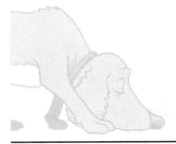

"Happiness Is..."

Training Philosophy and Terminology 1

The fully trained tracking dog has the unique ability to use his highly developed olfactory system to accomplish that which we cannot do, that is — to unerringly follow the footprints of a total stranger who has passed through an area hours before and identify any objects that he may have dropped along the way. For a dog to follow his master's footprints is natural, but to follow those of a stranger's path is the result of training. What it is that the dog actually smells when following the track of another human being is still not known and is under continuous scrutinization, but the fact that the dog can follow another human being, even hours after the fact is not in dispute at all. As a matter of fact, this unique ability of the dog to be able to identify certain scents that are not discernable to human beings has been utilized over the years in training dogs to discern various drugs, weapons, bombs, metals, gas leaks in pipelines and many other areas while the trainers were at a loss as to just what and how the dog managed to do this.

Training a dog in scent work, be it tracking (following the scent left by another person) or detecting a particular substance, is unlike training a dog for any other type of work, be it obedience, man work or any other physically oriented type of training. In scent work we do not know how the dog functions, nor do we ever know for certain whether or not the dog is, in

---

fact, performing his task correctly or not. In all of the areas of training that can be considered physical in nature, we can see and hear the dog as he progresses through his training, and it is his behavior we are concerned with. Should his behavior exemplify that which we desire of him, we reward him, and should it not, we correct his behavior in one of many ways. In this manner, since the dog is a creature of habit, we reinforce the wanted behavior, and we attempt to discourage the unwanted behavior.

In scent work, we are never certain whether or not the dog has, in fact, detected the scent of the intended olfactory stimulus or not, and in many cases we have unintentionally rewarded unwanted behavior and corrected the proper behavior, resulting in a badly confused dog that may finally refuse to attempt the ordained tasks we have set for him. How much simpler would be the task of training dogs to respond correctly to an olfactory stimulus if we only knew how the dog used his olfactory system and could verify whether or not his responses were correct?

When I first became interested in tracking training, I began to attend tracking test after tracking test in an attempt to secure for myself the correct methods for training tracking dogs from those individuals that were competing. Much to my surprise, only about one dog in ten was actually able to qualify for his title. I had assumed that scent work would be natural for most dogs, and that the training should, in fact, be simple and the results easily obtained. For a dog to follow the track of a second individual for only a few hundred yards should have presented no problem at all, yet here were all of these "trained" tracking dogs failing such a simple test. Somehow, an awful lot of people were doing something wrong. Before I would allow myself to be caught up in the same errors, I had to determine what it was that so many people were doing wrong, and what it was that the successful trainers were doing correctly.

With pencil and paper in hand, I began to document the stories, theories and all of the "should have done," as well as those things you should never do when training or handling a tracking dog. Listening to the old-timers' accounts of their experiences and their theories could fill a book, but a close examination of these ideas showed that most of them were contradictory. It seemed as if they would theorize in one manner when a dog performed in a certain manner, and later, when the same dog performed differently, the theory would suddenly change. No one seemed in agreement as to how the dog was actually using his nose, and no one seemed to want to agree with each other on what was creating a dog's problems. A dog in trouble at a tracking test was the result of the conditions (wind, sun, type of vegetation), bad handling (the old timers would have handled the dog differently), or bad luck. No one seemed to question the fact that perhaps the problem was the result of improper training.

When it came to the T.D.X. (Tracking Dog Excellent) tests, the prime requirement for a dog to qualify was luck. It was their consensus that the competing dogs needed "luck" in getting across the cross tracks. If this philosophy was correct, then why did the majority of participating dogs receive the disqualification whistle before the first turn, why did other dogs continue past the first turn with no indication that there was a turn, and why were some dogs not even working the three hour old track with their heads down? The only conclusion I could come up with was either the TDX type of track was too difficult for the average dog to handle, or they had not been properly trained for such an endeavor.

I quickly discovered that while everyone seemed to have a different explanation on what a dog was actually doing when following a track, no one seemed to have any logical approach to training dogs in tracking. You simply laid a short track, ran the dog on it, and gradually increased the length and number of turns in the track, but no one seemed to have heard of a program that would effectively teach all dogs to track. The only documentation on tracking training was the occasional chapter allocated to tracking in books on obedience training methods. The methods for training dogs in obedience were extensive, but the actual training methods to teach dogs tracking were virtually non-existent.

At this time, I made the decision that if I wanted to actually learn how to train dogs in tracking, I would have to research the area myself. This would necessitate the running experiments to test all of the theories and stories I had heard, to actually do those things I was told you just don't do, and, from the information obtained and documented, coming up with an actual training program to train dogs in tracking. During this period of testing and experimentation, I made the simple discovery that quickly led me into designing an effective training program that has enabled us to produce very capable tracking dogs, regardless of breed, in a few short months. It really didn't matter whether or not I could understand how, or what, a dog smelled when he was tracking. What really mattered was his behavior when placed in a particular situation.

For example, I discovered that most dogs had the tendency to circle to their right when arriving at a turn in the track. They also seemed to want to turn to the right (clockwise) when changing direction in their search for a ball, or when they started to lie down. I have no idea why this phenomena should occur with most dogs, but the reason for it is immaterial. Consider the importance of this behavior when attempting to teach a dog to take his first turn on a track. In order to ensure that he isn't going to lose the track for any length of time, we should be making his first turn to the right, so he will quickly pick up the new direction before he becomes bored, distracted or gives up. Armed with the knowledge obtained from dogs' behavioral responses under many different situations, plus the fact that the training should be geared for behavioral responses, we laid out the first training program and had the first dog's title in four short weeks of training. More experimentation followed, plus the documentation which had led to the present program contained in this book, which has resulted in 100% of all dogs completing the program, attaining their tracking title.

In the many years that followed the first implementation of the tracking program, certain things stood out in my mind as being critical features of any training program for tracking dogs and had created in me a certain philosophy toward tracking training, in general. What a dog smells, or how scent behaves, or just what scent is, should not even enter the novice's mind when attempting to train a dog in tracking. The only important thing is the type of behavior desired in the finished product of a handler - dog team. The ideal dog should follow the track with his nose to the ground in a steady, progressive rate of speed, varying no more than a few feet from the track itself. A dog that wanders, or quarters excessively, is not tracking properly. Indications of turns should be given within a few yards of the turn, and the dog should immediately engage in the quest for the track's new direction. The handler should not be simply an interested spectator holding onto the lead, but rather an observant assistant to the dog and responsive to the behavior of the dog. Both the handler and the dog must be taught how to react when placed into the many situations that can occur on a track.

The dog must be taught how to handle all of the possible obstacles he may encounter on a track, and the handler must be taught not only how to correctly interpret his dog, but also what specific actions to take when a certain problem arises on the track. No dog will ever make the TDX type of track by himself. It requires a man-dog team in every sense of the word. The training of such a team must begin with the idea that they are in training for TDX right from the beginning, not just for TD. The methods used to prepare such a team must be geared to encompass all of the problems they would find in both TD and TDX from the first day and throughout the entire training program.

To put a dog on a track simply for the sake of doing a track when the tracking team is in training is, in itself, a worthless exercise, for it accomplishes nothing. Every single track must have a definite purpose. Its layout must be designed for a very specific reason, and a definite objective in mind. Design of the track should be completed before the handler goes out to the fields to track, and the handler must be made aware of the significance of the track's purpose before he puts his dog on it. A properly designed and laid out track is to teach either the dog or handler (or both) something specific, and if it isn't, then they are going out simply for the exercise.

One of the reasons tracking training is so different from any other form of training is that this type of training must be totally free of compulsion. You cannot force a dog to track if he doesn't want to track. Dogs that receive punishment or scolding when they are learning to track, soon realize that as long as

---

their nose is pointing down at the ground they are safe from their handler's abuse, and they will take their master for a merry walk in a straight line, even if there is no track there to follow. This "pretend" type of tracking is a very commonplace behavior exhibited by dogs compulsively trained to track, and they are unreliable tracking dogs, at best.

Dog training methods are classified as compulsive, inducing, or a combination of both. Compulsive training utilizes varying degrees of physical force, pain and fear with the emphasis on corrections administered for unwanted behavior. Usually successful in diminishing unwanted behaviors, it has also been used with great success in training dogs for obedience competitions, creating a dog that is highly responsive to the handler's directions, but at the same time, diminishing his ability to work on his own without constant direction. Those dogs that have received the greatest amount of compulsive training for obedience competitions have had the greatest difficulty learning to track in comparison to those dogs with no previous training.

By appealing to a dog's senses, instincts and character, we can provide him with a reason to behave in a specific manner. The emphasis is placed on positive reinforcement of the wanted behavior, but not rewarding (nor correcting) unwanted behavior. This is inducive training, responsible for producing great circus dogs capable of complex routines, scenting dogs of all types working out areas with minimal direction, and the best, most reliable tracking dogs. No other method could have produced leak detection dogs after only two days of intensive training before being successfully used on a buried pipeline.

Both inducive and compulsive methods have their place and used properly will work. I cannot, however, envisage anyone teaching a dog to walk tightropes eight feet above the ground while carrying a raw egg through compulsion, nor can I picture anyone teaching two aggressive dogs not to fight through inducement.

Obedience training permits corrections to be effectively used, since the trainer can see, hear and feel unwanted behavior when it occurs. In scent work, the dogs are asked to perform something that the trainer cannot see, hear or feel, and whether the dog is actually performing correctly or not cannot be accurately deduced since the vagaries of scent are, as yet, a mystery. One correction applied when the dog is actually performing correctly could have a lasting detrimental effect.

Avoidance behavior is the direct result of totally compulsive methods that has a tremendous psychological impact when applied with sufficient force. Food refusal by dogs left unattended requires that the dog experience a violent fear-creating episode when attempting to pick up food thrown into his area in order to prevent poisoning. On the other hand, it is my own personal belief that any desirable behavior can be created in the dog by totally inducive methods, but very few trainers have the knowledge or experience necessary to implement such a training program. For this reason, most successful trainers use a combination of inducive and compulsive training methods.

Positive reinforcement is a reward the dog looks forward to and enjoys, and the greater the psychological impact of the reward, the faster a response is learned. The reward may be physical or psychological in nature, such as food, play, praise or that which appeals to sexual instincts or the desire to pursue and fight. Positive reinforcers, such as food, to the satisfied dog, or praise to the dog having no craving whatever for human companionship will have little effect, but deprivation of either from dogs that like their food or companionship will enhance their effectiveness.

The process of creating a desired response to a command involves two distinct processes, teaching and training. When attempting to initiate a correct response for the first time, the handler is involved with teaching. Once the response is obtained and the dog has obviously learned the correct response, the process of making the desired behavior consistent is a function of training. Food, when utilized as a "teaching tool" correctly, is excellent as a positive reinforcer. However, no other aid is as badly abused as food. When using food, the trainer should use it on a fixed ratio schedule (used every time a correct response is elicited) and when training, use it on a variable ratio schedule (a random number of correct responses) so that the dog is never sure when he will receive the physical reinforcement. In this manner, a word of praise is substituted for the physical reward until the dog receives a physical reward, perhaps once in 1,000 responses. In a comparison between compulsive versus inducive methods, psychologists have discovered that the rate of extinction of a learned response is slower when the animal learned through the application of positive reinforcers as opposed to negative reinforcers.

The "key" to successful tracking training is in motivating the dog, creating in him the desire to "want" to track. Trained properly, the dog should have a strong desire to track instilled in him by the trainer throughout his training program. To correct a dog for undesired behavior when teaching him to track is a commonplace error or inexperienced handlers because you just don't know what the problem might be. Perhaps the dog has a nasal irritation and cannot detect any odor to follow. Medication might have been administered to the dog in the past few days that is affecting his olfactory or mental processes. There may be several hundred reasons why the dog is physically incapable of tracking when he receives the correction. Worse yet, perhaps the dog has picked up the scent of another track laid minutes before you arrived to track, and now you are scolding him for doing what "he" thinks is the correct thing to do. In any case, he knows what he is, or isn't, doing. You, the handler, can only guess, and that type of guessing is invariably wrong.

There is always a reason for a dog's apparent difficulty on track, and should it persist, you should stop tracking for the day. There is no possible way for you to understand his reason for having stopped tracking, and should you believe that it is because the dog is lazy, bored, or just plain not interested, then don't blame the dog for your failure to make it interesting and fun to do. Too many people become angry when they lose patience, taking out their frustrations on their dog, resulting in the dog's learning to fear and hate tracking. We have discovered that the administration of certain medications can have side effects that impair the dog's ability to smell or to concentrate on a track. Should a dog suddenly stop tracking, it is wise to sit down and ask yourself, "What has happened to my dog in the past week that would be different from the week before?" which will often give you the answer to why he has stopped tracking. With a few days rest, he may just snap out of it.

One of the greatest failures of handlers occurs when they first get the dog out of the car in that insufficient time is allowed for the dog to "clear his head" from the constant fumes present in the car. The dog should be given sufficient time to adequately void and have a bowel movement before being put on a track. Should the dog stop to urinate or have a bowel movement when on a track, simply stop and allow him time to finish his ablutions before commanding him to resume the track. Most dogs will have this tendency to void on the track because of the strenuous nature of this form of training. A dog that has been confined for a period of time, and then is asked to exercise strenuously will invariable have to have a bowel movement. Males do, however, have a fascination for trees, stumps, and fence posts, which should not be tolerated when tracking. This business of "leaving their mark" should be discouraged by the handler right from the start of tracking training. Should he suddenly break off tracking, or stop searching for a track to head for such a tempting spot with his head up, then verbally scold him with a stern "NO" in no uncertain terms, but do not jerk him on the tracking line.

Scolding does have its place when tracking training is underway, but should never be used when the dog makes a mistake or stops working. Should he become momentarily distracted by something, allow him time to satiate his curiosity and try to refocus his attention on the track he was following. If he continues to focus his attention on something else, then it is time to verbally scold him with a stern "NO." If he simply stops tracking, or should he simply quit and stand there looking up at you, or if he seems unable to locate the track, then it is time to encourage him as much as possible. Point to the track while you take him step by step down the track and attempt to excite him about the presence of the track.

Tracking training is physically tiring work for the dog since he has to cover uneven ground while concentrating on the one odor he is following, regulate his breathing pattern to accommodate adequate scenting and often pull his handler behind him. For this reason, it is advisable for handlers to bring along with them a container of drinking water, plus a drinking dish for the dog. The water contained in the container should be from the dog's area since a change in drinking water can have the same effect on a dog as it will on the handler, in that diarrhea might be induced. In order to make the work a little easier on the dog (and the handler), all tracking training should be performed in the early morning hours of spring, summer and fall. The summer months, in particular, become very hot around mid-day and should be avoided when in the early stages of training, for the heat can really discourage a dog and can result in his constantly looking for a shady place to retreat to. Once he is performing well on aged tracks, he can be worked during the hotter parts of the day in preparation for TDX. For the handler's peace of mind, I'd suggest a complete rubberized outfit similar in style to that worn by fishermen in bad weather, plus a generous supply of mosquito repellent.

Most tracking training occurs in the "green" time of the year when the mosquito problem is at its worst. More dogs are being lost due to heartworm now than ever before, and this problem has been constantly on the move north. It can now be found in most of the United States and Canada. Dogs should be constantly protected when possible from mosquito bites, since they are the intermediary hosts of this problem and should never be kept out in a mosquito-infested area longer than necessary. Periodic examinations should be made for this parasite under a veterinarian's direction, and, if necessary, the dog placed on the preventative as prescribed by a veterinarian. Be prepared for olfactory problems when the preventative is first administered and for a few weeks after.

Sometimes a dog may be of the type that will deliberately take a break when actively engaged in following a track. He will seem to deliberately stop tracking, look around, proceed to the end of the line out to one side of the track and relieve himself. Then, with great deliberation, he'll proceed right back to where he left the track and resume his efforts in pursuing the track. In this manner, he has given himself a break and shouldn't be criticized for it, since he resumes his efforts within a few moments. In the tracking portions of the Schutzhund examination he'll be penalized for such a display, but when on a TDX type of track, or when in actual pursuit of a real track where he may have to track for periods of over a mile, then it is a natural thing for him to relieve himself and continue on.

It becomes quite obvious, even to the novice student of tracking what specific behavior is consistent with his dog when he is actually following a track. When there is an abrupt deviation from this behavior, the handler must become aware of the possibility that the dog is no longer following a track. Coming to a complete halt when in doubt will often prompt the dog to stop and look back at the handler, and if there is no track at that point, he will probably start casting for it. If the track is, in fact, still there, he will probably resume tracking, and, if properly trained, will respond to a tightening lead by settling into the harness with a strong pull. Should there be an article there that the dog has stopped to sniff, the handler must acknowledge the find, for the dog is, in fact, trying to tell him something. Should the dog's behavior be such that he never wags his tail when following a track, and then suddenly it begins to wag furiously, the handler should be aware of the fact that the dog may have discovered a field mouse, and be prepared to issue a stern "NO."

Selections of Articles

Another important consideration when commencing with a tracking program is the selection of articles to be used. During the initial stages of training, you should use a random selection of articles, preferably made of leather, easily obtained from any shoemaker's shop, plus a couple of non-leather articles. Use a different article on each track in order to get the dog used to expecting almost anything at the end of the track. Later on in the program, you should start including handkerchiefs, socks, pen cases, business cards, etc. One dog entered in a TD test several years ago performed exceptionally well on his track, but failed to indicate the article which happened to be a pen case the track layer had dropped, because he had forgotten to take the assigned glove with him. The dog was failed. However, the handler argued strongly and was reassigned another track which his dog refused to track. Had this dog been trained to indicate any article dropped by the track layer, he would have obtained his title, but, as fate would have it, he did not.

Preparedness

Lack of preparedness is another failing of a great number of handlers, especially at tracking competitions. Some handlers spend time as a spectator at the events they are entered in rather than ensuring that they are ready when called to start their track. Before they are called, they should have taken the dog out of the car and exercised him, ensured that their tracking line is straightened out, and that the dog has had the time to clear his head. I once witnessed a handler who tangled his tracking line around the wheels of a parked car. He started the track with his line in a massive tangle and actually dropped the line while attempting to untangle it, as the dog was moving on the track. He ended up at an insane run to try to catch his line as the dog began to run the track. These requirements should be practiced every day of training so that they are a conditioned behavior on the part of the handler by the time he is ready for a competition.

Before advancing toward the track, ensure the tracking line is straightened out, the collar and lead put away and then, simply use the line as a lead and collar by wrapping the line around the dog's neck and snapping it onto itself. In this manner you'll have no problems resulting from collars and leads. Place the harness on the dog before you arrive at the starting flag, and when you start, handle him the way you always did during training.

While you're on the track, don't talk him to death, and when his drive wanes, encourage him, and don't just let him work with ever decreasing drive. During the test, the tracking dog tells his handler everything. Trust your dog, believe him, and don't attempt to use logic.

During the actual training of the dog in tracking, there are only a few key points that will ensure rapid, visible progress. First, we have to motivate the dog — give him a reason to look for something that is out in that field; secondly, to have him believe us when we say it is out there; and thirdly, the easiest and swiftest way to find it is to follow that strange odor which always lead to the desired item out there. The only tools we have to work with are the motivational force we use, and the actual track itself. We can design the track he is to follow in countless ways, but the only successful design is the one that is conducive to his learning. Each time we design a track, we must attempt to teach the dog, in a simple ascending order, a series of objectives that he can easily master and the mastery of each objective must be visible to us. It seems ludicrous to me that anyone would expect a dog to master the twentieth step before he has mastered the first nineteen steps. It is a very logical progression for teaching a dog to track that I advocate in this book, and it has yet to fail me.

Scent Work in General

Tracking training is only one small area of scent work with which this book is concerned. Training dogs for any of the other areas, such as identification of narcotics, marijuana, foresight (as the prime ingredient in bombs) or weapon detection (burnt cordite) is essentially the same. Here, however, the dog is taught to recognize one particular odor and is taught how to react when this scent is discerned. Detection of buried human beings, specific metals or the butyl mercaptans used in pipeline leak detection is also the same when it comes to looking for a specific odor, and the dogs are once again taught a specific method of identification. In the training of the dogs to look for a specific odor, there is very little difference. However, the method of identification will vary from each specific odor to each specific odor.

For example, in tracking, it really doesn't matter how the dog identifies the article he discovers. He may retrieve it to the handler. He may sit when he finds it, or he may lie down. He may bark at it, or he may simply stand and look at it. Any of the mentioned methods of identification are acceptable at any competition involving tracking, whether it's Canadian, American or Schutzhund tracking. These methods of identification would not be acceptable for some of the other areas of scent work. In fact, some of these methods of identification would be hazardous, or else ineffective. Who would want their dog to retrieve, for example, a live bomb, or to bark loudly when a weapon is discerned by the dog in a war zone, or to simply lie down when in a room known to harbor narcotics?

In 1974, I was commissioned to train dogs to search for and locate leaks in a brand new natural gas pipeline that was to be opened in nine days from the time I was approached. However, the consulting engineering firm that designed the line knew there were leaks in the line and had attempted, unsuccessfully, to locate these leaks with every instrument know to modern technology. The 12" diameter pipeline, 94 miles in length, had been hydrostatically tested up to 2,000 pounds per square inch and would explode a section of line before they could locate the leak. Somehow, they had heard about the uncanny ability of dogs to discern even the slightest traces of odors which they had been trained to locate, and were prepared to give the dogs a try. This meant nine days in which to complete a training program and to employ the dogs successfully over this 94-mile stretch of pipeline, which was buried at least six feet deep under wet, heavy clay. The task seemed formidable, but I was certain it could be done, as long as I started the training with dogs
that knew already how to use their noses to locate a designated scent.

I decided to use three dogs and their handlers on the basis of:
1. Availability
2. The distinctive types of training each dog had already received in "scent work"
3. The dog's proven record in its field of scent work and learning rates

The first dog selected was a young German Shepherd male, "Guardian Admiral Mike," owned and handled by Ilene Newman of Kingsville, Ontario. This dog was an accomplished TDX dog, having earned all of his North American Tracking titles. He had been trained to a Utility Dog level, and his handler was knowledgeable in scent work and as a handler of tracking dogs.

The second dog selected was also a German Shepherd Dog, "Kaiser," owned and handled by Denis Pardue of Windsor, Ontario. This dog had received no tracking training at all, but was a very accomplished "Free and Directed Searching Dog," capable of quartering over a 100 yard wide area under his handler's direction, while using all of his senses to discover objects either dropped or thrown by other human beings. This dog had been trained to CDX, but had never competed in licensed competition.

The third dog was my own German Shepherd Dog "Avenger," who had already proven his proficiency in both obedience and tracking by earning every obedience and tracking title in North America. In "Free and Directed Search," he was as accomplished as the second choice dog, "Kaiser." Now I had one excellent tracking dog, one excellent searching dog, and one dog that was proficient in both areas of scent work to start the training. Should one type of background prove to be more advantageous than the other, I should still end up with at least two dogs that could work the pipeline effectively.

The dog that demonstrated the highest degree of success during the training program was "Kaiser," the searching dog, yet after the first week on the pipeline, this same dog proved to be the least successful in finding the actual leaks, and we had to discontinue using him. The other two dogs were highly successful, with my own dog completing the line with a 100% record, while the other dog, "Mike," found the smallest of the leaks. It is interesting to note that the method of actual search employed on the line was the "Directed Search."

I formulated the training program along the same lines as the tracking training program, based upon behavioral objectives, and within two and one-half days, we were ready for the pipeline. We could take the dogs for a walk along any unknown area and have the dogs break away from us when they caught wind of ten parts per million of the butyl mercaptan odorant, even when it was deposited on a rusting tin can, or when it was buried several feet beneath the ground. In this case, we had taught the dogs to believe that when they caught scent of the mercaptan odorant, there was an article buried underground. They had been taught to respond by digging furiously at the source of the scent. We now had seven days in which to use the dogs to search for leaks along the 94-mile pipeline.

The first twenty-mile stretch of pipeline selected for our test run had been searched many times before with electronic, chemical and sonic detectors, but to no avail. The line was still registering an eight-pound per twenty-four hour leak. The construction workers employed to test the line anticipated possible three leaks, which would account for this pressure loss in twenty-four hours. In the first day, the dogs identified more than twenty possible leaks, which no one was prepared to agree with. The next day, when fifteen leaks had been verified by digging up those sections of pipeline identified by the dogs as possessing leaks, all doubts had been erased. From that point on, no

Kaiser, Avenger and *Mike,* the Leak Detection Trio

one doubted the accuracy, or the ability, of the dogs. By the time we had covered the line three times, over one hundred and fifty confirmed leaks had been detected by the dogs.

During this period of working the pipeline, many unusual things occurred, which substantiated my belief that we really do not know, nor can we really understand, the olfactory prowess of the dog. For example, take the one incident where one dog identified a section of pipe as having a leak, when it was less

Avenger discovering a leak in a buried natural gas pipeline

than 860 pounds per square inch pressure and was buried eighteen feet beneath the surface with a mound of heavy clay over the top of it that was several feet in height. When this section was uncovered, no leak could be found, although there was a faint, lingering smell of the mercaptan present. The hole was left uncovered, and when the pressure was raised to 1500 pounds per square inch, they managed to locate the leak — three weeks after the dog had first discerned it.

When I was working my own dog by directing his quartering from right to left across the pipeline when working directly into the wind, I crossed a concession road into the next farmer's field. The farmer was in the process of finishing his plowing. The entire field had just been plowed and you could not tell which direction the pipeline ran. I took a hasty look behind me at the test leads that protrude above the pipeline at each roadway and tried to pinpoint ahead of me the direction that the line should take. Casting my dog across the supposed line, as I had done before, I figured there should be no real problem — until my dog began to change his direction of quartering and began what appeared to me as a right hand, 90 degree turn. I doublechecked to make sure he was, in fact, disobeying my direction and decided that I might as well let him proceed, even though I was certain he was in error. Imagine my surprise when we arrived at the next concession road (each concession road was about one mile apart), and there were the test leads — dead center on his casting line. Somehow my dog had known that it was the pipeline he was following, and he had detected the turn by scent (certainly not by sight in the freshly plowed field) and was committed to following it.

Nearing the end of our search, I was suddenly faced with another situation that I knew not how to handle. Ahead of me like an advancing armada were the "clean up crews," comprised of several bulldozers, graders and men. Should I wait for them to pass? Would my dog be able to work the area immediately after they had flattened the roach (a ridge covering the pipeline), or would the heavy equipment disturb his train of thought when he had to look for that single odorant? I decided to continue working my dog until it became obvious that he was either distracted by the equipment, or until I could no longer figure out a way around them? He continued his search, right up to the blade of the first oncoming bulldozer, then around it to continue the search behind it. "Do you really think your dog can find a leak by the equipment?" shouted a dozer operator. "What does he do when he finds a leak?" questioned another. Just then my dog stopped his search and began to dig furiously behind the second bulldozer — sure enough, another leak!

During the end of our training period we were using clothespins that had been sterilized (to eliminate human odor) and anointed with ten parts per million of the butyl mercaptan odorant which we dropped into narrow holes made by piercing the ground with half inch diameter stakes. Once we buried them by closing the holes made by the stakes, we would practice the dogs over the area so that they could be successful in digging up the planted articles. Since we wanted the dogs to be successful on their first day, we had people move out ahead of us on the pipeline with instructions to bury the pegs, as in our training, every several hundred paces. In this manner we hoped to keep up the dogs' interest, while searching continuously for ten to sixteen hours at a stretch. The dogs had no difficulty in locating the pegs, along with the many leaks they found. When we came back for the second and third times over the line, I was astonished when the dogs would break away from the pipeline to zero in on these pegs that we had thrown away three weeks before. I decided that here was an opportunity to obtain an exact measure of how much scent the dogs were actually detecting, since I taught at a college and could have the chemical department analyze the pegs and tell me how much of the butyl mercaptan was actually remaining on the pegs. Once again I was astonished when they came back to inform me that they could not detect any mercaptan on the peg, and that the dogs had to be better than one part per trillion in their olfactory work — and that was at distances over forty feet away.

By the time we had completed the pipeline three times, the dogs had successfully detected over 150 leaks, 4 leaky valves (one of them over 12 feet above the ground) through snowstorms, 0 degree weather, quicksand (one handler had to be physically dug out of it), and over rivers, highways and plowed fields. The smallest leak was microscopic, buried 18 feet deep, and the dogs had to work continuously from daybreak to dark. The handlers covered up to fifteen miles each day (the dogs up to sixty miles per day), while the dogs were asked to work at all times and concentrate exclusively on looking for that one scent. I doubt very much if I will ever see dogs work so hard and so faithfully again in my lifetime, and it was both an experience and an education to see such fidelity in a dog. There is no doubt in my mind that these animals would never have learned so quickly, nor performed so well if they hadn't been trained inducively, without corrections. Also, it never ceases to amaze me when I consider how many times the dogs were correct in what they were doing, and we would have been wrong if we had used our own intelligence to determine if they were right or wrong. Once again, it reinforced my belief that we do not know how, nor what it is exactly that the dog smells when using this unusual olfactory power that he possesses.

The dog not only possesses this ability to detect scents that are not perceptible to man, but to follow the scent right back to its source. Humans can detect many odors, but this ability to zero in on the actual source of the odor still escapes man. Early in our search for pipeline leaks, two specific incidents highlighted this unique ability on the part of the dog. When we spilled about half a cup of the butyl mercaptan (which smells roughly like skunk) on a neighbor's lawn, we discovered several individuals from the gas company, searching for the source of the gas on their hands and knees (They suspected a gas line leak in the city, and were called in to investigate.). They never did locate the source, even though you could smell the foul odor a block away. When my own dog discovered one of the first actual leaks in the pipeline, I got down on my stomach, and by placing my nose in the exact spot where he had dug, I could faintly detect the odorant myself. I placed a marker flag a few inches away from the hole he dug and asked the superintendent to verify it. He placed his nose at the spot I had marked, only a few inches away from the spot where the dog had dug, and could not detect any odorant. When I asked him to smell the actual place where the dog had dug, he could distinctly smell the odorant. These sort of things simply reinforce my belief that we do not know how, nor what it is that the dog smells, nor do we really have any objective understanding of how he uses his nose, but this lack of understanding is no hindrance when we are concerned only with behavior, and it is a type of behavior that we are attempting to elicit from the dog when we are attempting to train him in scent work.

The type of behavior we are concerned with here is that of the ideal tracking dog, how he should behave when on a track in competition for his tracking title, and not for any other specialized area of scent work. It is toward this idea that this book is intended. We want a dog that will, by the end of the training program, navigate a TD or a TDX type of track with his nose down on the track as if it were tied to a rail, never deviating more than a few feet from the track and identifying any object recently dropped by the track layer. We want a dog that will "want" to track, a dog that will not be distracted by anything occurring about him, and one that will not lose his concentration, even when he overshoots a turn. We want a dog to believe he is right when on the track, and one that is prepared to pull his handler off his feet if he is doubtful about continuing after the dog. All of this is a product of correct training methods.

Defining Terms of Behavior and Scent

We really do not have very much knowledge when it comes right down to understanding just what it is the tracking dog actually is following when actively engaged in following the track of another human being. Experiments that have been conducted in the past were limited in scope, lacking in details and performed with only a limited number of dogs. These experiments did, however, prompt several theories involving the dog's olfactory system, and those theories were then tested again, but the information obtained is still quite inconclusive. We can, however, observe the behavioral habits of the fully trained dog when on track and placed in certain controlled situations to see how he will respond. When we see almost 100% of these trained dogs reacting in the same manner to a

---

given situation, we can then form certain conclusions regarding his behavior when faced with the same situation again. Some of these experiments, which were of great value to us in formulating a training program, are discussed in detail in the next chapter.

In order to understand these experiments and later, the actual training program itself, we must have a basic understanding of the terminology which I will be using throughout this book. Here then are the terms with which I will be describing the behavior of dogs when using their noses to find a human being and the behavior of scent as I envisage it.

Track Scent

When a person, animal or object moves through an area by coming in contact with the ground, the vegetation is crushed (or damaged) wherever the person, animal or object comes in contact with the ground. This disturbed area at the point of contact will have a different odor than the undisturbed area surrounding it. This "different" scent, or odor where the area has been disturbed is what I call "track scent." Track scent will take a very long time to reduce to nothing and may be increased by moisture, such as a light rain, heavy dew, light snow, or time of day. In the early morning, when the sun is rising and the temperature is increasing, causing evaporation, the track scent will seem to strengthen as if the scent is being pulled upward to a point where the dog can more easily detect it. Should the weather conditions be just right, for example, a foggy atmosphere with no sun, cool air and virtually no wind, the track scent may linger for days.

Extreme heat, on the other hand, with a good stiff breeze will cause the track scent to become undetectable in a very short period of time. A light rain occurring after a period of high heat has the tendency to freshen the track scent and make it more detectable to the dog a short time after the rain than it was just before the rain. In order to better understand just what I mean by track scent, think of a compost pile on a farm, which has been undisturbed for a long period of time. You can approach the compost heap on a very hot day without really getting a good smell of it, as long as the hard crust hasn't been disturbed. Should you break the crust with a long pole, you will get an immediate smell of purification from the area broken, which certainly does not smell of a human being, or of the pole used to break the crust. This, then, would compare vaguely with the term "track scent."

Body Odor

When a human being touches or handles an item, he imparts his own scent to the article he has touched. Over the years, many dogs have proven without question their ability to not only detect this individual body odor, but also have been taught to indicate or retrieve only that article which possesses the particular body odor they have been taught to identify. This can be seen by anyone interested in watching the scent discrimination exercises in Utility classes at obedience trials. When a person walks through an area, he will leave his body odor on anything he comes in contact with. This body odor will combine with the track scent where the person has walked, forming a sort of "perfume" (for the lack of a better term), which will consist of the track scent, body odor, and odor of the particular footwear and clothing that has come into contact with any part of the traveled area. This combination then is the combination of (1) track scent and (2) body odor.

Airborne Scent

When an individual is upwind of the dog, he can be detected easily by the dog's sense of smell through his body odor that is being carried by the moving currents of air. Once the individual has passed through an area, his body odor will be carried to many different areas where it may be captured by ditches, potholes, tree lines, etc. Later, the changes in wind may cause this trapped body odor to be released where it is the "Airborne Scent." The combination of the track scent and the body odor will likewise be carried by the wind many yards off the actual track left by the individual. That scent, which is carried by the airborne currents is what I call "Airborne Scent."

Scent Strength

From the moment a person walks through an area, the strength of the airborne scent, the body odor, and the track scent begin to diminish. The first to become undetectable is the airborne scent, the second to go is the body odor, and last of all to disappear is the track scent itself. Since the track scent lasts the longest, and because the tracking dog that is trying for a TDX title must go onto a track that is over three hours old, we must teach the dog to detect and follow the track scent rather than the body odor, or airborne scent of an individual. Dogs that are working for police departments within the city, on the other hand, should be taught to follow body odor and utilize airborne scent whenever it is available. When properly trained, the TDX type of dog should be capable of following the track scent, body odor or airborne scent.

When we are specifically training dogs as "tracking dogs," primarily for competition, rather than as "trailers" (followers of body odor), we lay the tracks out in such a manner so as to encourage the dog to follow very close to the track rather than several yards away. The observable behavior exhibited by dogs following an individual that has passed through an area can be classified as trailing, fringe following or tracking. These terms apply to where, in the field of scent surrounding the track, the dog places himself when following a track. (See figure 1)

Tracking Dogs

The tracking dogs follow very closely to the actual track with their noses to the track and never track with their heads up. The "loss of track" indications are easily observed even by the most novice spectators as well as their discovery of a track. Their pattern of following a track seldom deviates more than a few feet off the actual track, and when they arrive at a turn, they seldom overshoot the turn by more than a few yards. More often than not, they will seldom circle at a turn, but will instead discover the new direction of the track with little actual searching. They become so engrossed in the track scent that they become oblivious to normal distractions encountered on a track.

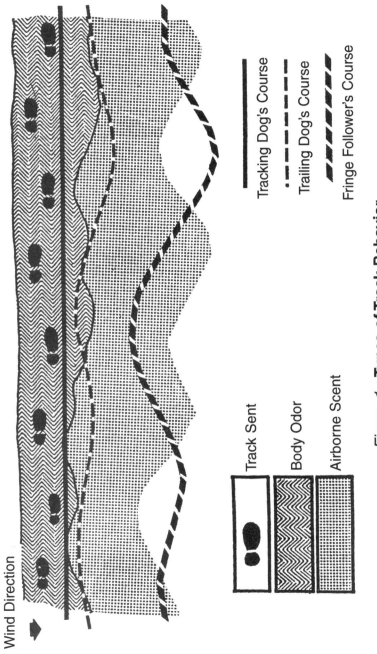

Figure 1 • **Types of Track Behavior**

Trailing Dogs

The trailing dogs follow the body odor with their heads down when tracking with the wind, but lift their heads when tracking into the wind and half way down when in a crosswind. With a crosswind, they will follow the track a distance downwind of the actual track with a slight tendency to quarter downwind of the actual track. It is not unusual to see trailing dogs follow a track as much as ten to twenty yards downwind of the actual track. When arriving at a turn when the wind is blowing at their backs, the dogs' tendency to overshoot is pronounced and reading their "loss of track" indication is sometimes very difficult since their course is rather erratic with considerable quartering. They are easily distracted by normal distractions and have the tendency to want to check things out by sight.

Fringe Followers

This type of dog seems to follow selected scent strength - normally where the scent has already dispersed to a determined level of strength. On the track, their behavior shows a great deal more quartering than the trailing dogs although they seldom quarter across the track itself when in a crosswind. They will quarter across the apparent scent strength level they are following. This can be a real problem if it is developed in the dogs through training and can result in the dogs following the scent strength level a long distance off the actual track when tracking with the wind at their back. Should they overshoot the turn, they could find themselves many yards off the turn and be greeted by a change in wind direction that makes it impossible to relocate the track. The fringe followers are very easily distracted and rather difficult to restart. Their minds are seldom on the track, and they track in spurts.

Figure 2 indicates the normal behavior of the three types of tracking dogs when placed on identical racks with a wind condition of 5 - 10 miles per hour in the direction shown.

In the case of the tracking dog, he is following the track scent very close to the actual track, since there just isn't much scent on the downwind side of the track. He notices a change in track scent easily when arriving at a turn. The dog will usually

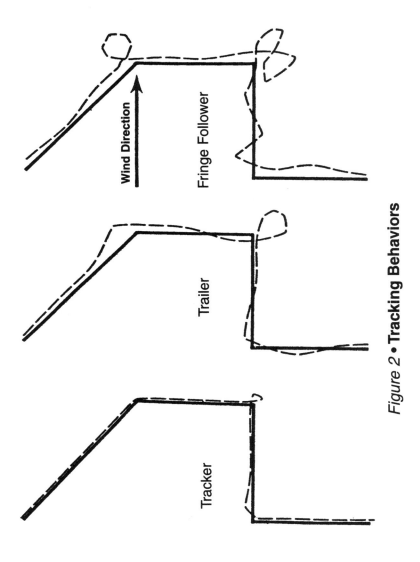

Wind Direction

Fringe Follower

Trailer

Tracker

Figure 2 • **Tracking Behaviors**

indicate loss of track positively enough for the handler to notice and come to a halt with the actual turn being somewhere between the handler and the dog. This can be a great advantage when participating at a tracking test - to be confident that the new direction of the track will always be in front of you somewhere.

The trailer, on the other hand, will follow the track much further downwind where he can distinguish the body odor from the track scent. When he gets too close to the track, he cannot distinguish the body odor from the track scent, and he will immediately begin to cast downwind once more to pick up the body odor again. He carries past the corner before detecting any loss of track and will indicate the corners much later than will the tracker, especially when trailing with a wind blowing in the same direction as he is tracking. The handler will read the dog's indication of "loss of track" at the corner or a short distance past the turn, which means that the dog has to cast behind the handler in order to locate the new direction of the track.

The fringe follower is working the track a long distance downwind of the actual track, swinging even further downwind, as the wind gusts strengthen, and veering back toward the track when the velocity decreases, giving him the impression of quartering. When he is tracking in the same direction as the wind is blowing, he overshoots the turn badly. He is so far off that the handler usually comes to a stop when he recognizes the "loss of track" indication a considerable distance from the corner. When this type of dog circles, he usually picks up the track somewhere behind the handler. A very strong, gusty wind will often result in the fringe follower's going as far as 30 - 50 yards off the track, and, should the wind direction change or stop altogether, he is so far off the track that he'll be unable to pick up the track again in his normal casting for it.

The Track Sure Dog

This type of tracking dog becomes so engrossed in what he is doing that he becomes oblivious to everything about him. Pheasants may explode from beneath him, rabbits and other game race in front of him, yet he continues to follow the track unperturbed. One such dog of mine came upon a cat sitting on the track in the middle of a 2700-yard track. Under normal situations, he would have instantly dispatched the cat or pursued it if it broke and ran. So engrossed was he in the track that he simply pushed the cat to one side and without breaking his stride, continued on about his business. This type of dog is usually not hyperactive, has a compulsive retrieving instinct and possesses a high degree of concentration. Another term used to describe this type of performance is a "track faithful" dog.

The Track Happy Dog

This type of dog's behavior is easily spotted, for he is easily distracted when following a track. His attention span is limited in whatever it is that he does, and his desire to work a track out varies from intense to minimal. He shows definite signs of hyperactivity, is constantly on the move when not working, and although he seems difficult to train, will respond with incredible speed to some learning situations. He is usually a heartbreaker at tracking tests, and should he attain his tracking title, he certainly lacks the necessary concentration and "stick-to-it-iveness" that is required to make his T.D.X. title.

Line Tracking

Line tracking is a behavior exhibited by the dog when following a track, that is learned during the initial stages of training and is very necessary if the dog is to become capable of following extended tracks. During the initial training of a dog, he can see the article being dropped by the track layer and he mentally marks where he thinks the article has been dropped. When he is sent after the article, he will run out to the spot he has marked in his memory, and once there, he puts his nose down to the ground in an attempt to locate it by scent. Normally, the location he has marked is short of the article, so he uses his nose to locate it, resulting in his detection of the track layer's scent, which he follows up to the article. The distance between the marked drop and the article increases, which results in the dog's using his nose for greater periods of time in order to locate the article. The dog soon begins to exhibit the characteristic trait of scenting for several yards, then lifting his head to look for the article while continuing in the general direction of the article for several paces before resorting to scenting once again. Sometimes he will forget what he is doing at this point, should he observe something else that catches his interest, and he has to be restarted on the track. Should he remember that he is tracking, he'll put his nose down and start once again. Gaining experience as time goes on, you'll notice that even though he is tracking all the way to the article, he will scent for several yards and, having determined the direction which the track has taken, will lift his head slightly, breathe normally for several paces and then begin to scent again without breaking pace. Within a few yards of his picking up the scent of the track, he will have determined direction, or what line the track has taken, and will now track by checking every few yards for the direction of the track by scent.

This characteristic can result in the dog's overshooting a corner should he not be scenting when he arrives at a turn. However, when on extended tracks of great distance, the dog should line track to a certain degree in order that he shouldn't completely exhaust himself. I have seen one dog that did not line track and was scenting all the way. By the time the dog had completed several hundred yards, he was frothing at the mouth and had to be stopped before he killed himself with exhaustion. The ideal tracker will learn to scent for a distance, and then carry on with normal breathing for a short distance before resuming scenting again, and the wise handler will permit this when on a long straight stretch of a track.

Step Tracking

Dogs that line track are common in TD competition, since the track is relatively fresh and laid in areas that are well vegetated. When the dog enters the world of TDX, the conditions of tracking change. There will be areas that contain no vegetation at all - perhaps plowed fields or generous areas of sand that he'll have to track over. More than three hours have elapsed since the track has been laid, and the only place the dog is going to detect any scent in this type of an area is where the

Figure 3 • **Line tracking**

Scenting   Exhale   Scenting

The Track Sure Dog

---

track layer's feet have actually come into contact with the ground. Line tracking in this situation would be hopeless. The dog must be taught to follow and look for each individual footstep if he is to navigate this portion of the track. Dogs that are step tracking will appear to be quartering with their head and shoulders only as they move from footstep to footstep.

In order to appreciate the difference between line tracking and step tracking, let's take an example I'm sure you'll be able to understand. Place a row of marbles on the floor of a room with each marble only one inch apart, and then darken the room and proceed to determine the direction of the marbles with your bare feet. Once you have determined the direction, you can easily step out with large steps and be successful in proceeding in the correct direction. Now try the same thing, but space each marble about two feet apart before trying it. In the first case, we have a similarity between line tracking and in the second case, a similarity between step tracking. The ideal type of tracking dog must have the ability to line track when feasible and to step track when necessary.

Terrain

The type of terrain and vegetation will have a distinct effect on the dog's behavior when learning to track, as well as on the experienced track sure dog. Should the track lead downhill, we can expect the dog to possibly overshoot a turn, simply because his momentum is difficult for him to stop. On the other hand, the dog that is tracking uphill will have the tendency to stop closer to the actual turn. Hills can have a profound effect on dogs just learning to track, since the wind and eddy currents can blow the track scent and body odor in many different directions, resulting in the beginning dogs wanting to quarter more than if they were tracking on the flat.

Tracks laid beside a tree line can result in strange behaviors being exhibited by dogs that are learning to track for the first time. The wind may be blowing toward the tree line when checked several feet above ground level. But when checked at ground level, you might discover that the movement of air is in the opposite direction as a result of an eddy current. I have witnessed one track that contained one turn that headed toward the tree line toward which the wind was blowing. When the dog was started, he headed from the starting stake directly to the article without even attempting to search for a track. When we tested the wind condition, we discovered that it was, in fact, blowing from the dog toward the tree line, but at ground level, it was blowing from the article directly to the dog, and he had simply headed directly toward the object of his search, which he could easily smell.

The tracking dog is seldom bothered by changes in wind, but will end up tracking anywhere from a few inches to a few feet on the downwind side of a track. The fringe follower and the trailing dog's performance will be drastically affected by such changes. Uneven ground area where ditches, potholes and clumps of high vegetation or trees will have an effect on the body odor they are following. Occasionally, these types of dogs will have the tendency to investigate depressions and ditches well off the actual track where body odor has collected. This can result in their leaving the actual track to a point of no return.

Changes in types of vegetation can cause the tracking dogs to exhibit a "look of track" indication when following a track that leads from one type of vegetation to another. For example, a dog that is tracking in a straight line through a wheat field will, when he enters a rye field, perform as if he has momentarily lost the scent. It seems rather logical to my way of thinking that the disturbed ground in a wheat field would smell different from the disturbed ground in a rye field. Should the dog be committed to following the original scent of disturbed wheat, he probably is looking for the same type of scent when he enters the rye field. While looking for the original scent in the rye field, he probably smells a myriad scents, and it takes him a moment or two to determine that this new scent is the correct one. Those dogs that are highly experienced and have been exposed to many such situations will take much less time in determining that the new scent is, in fact, the correct one. While it is wise to start training dogs for tracking in fields where changes in vegetation do not occur, they must be trained under conditions of vegetation changes once they are, in fact, tracking.

Going from a well-vegetated field into a plowed field seems to compound the problem, since not only has the original scent changed, but also he must now step track if the track has been aged. Training dogs to track in freshly plowed fields seems to present the dog with no problem as long as it is a "hot" track that hasn't been aged for any great length of time. As a matter of fact, the freshly plowed field is one area that appears to be better at retaining the scent than a short cropped grass (pasture) type of field.

Moisture

As I have mentioned before, very little in depth study has been made in regard to the olfactory powers of the dog and even less has been made into the actual effects of moisture on a track. It can, however, create a real problem for the trailing and fringing types of dogs. On a foggy, windless day with no appreciable amount of heat, the body odor seems to hang in the air and is distributed over a wide area off the actual track. Slowly it will disperse, saturating an area, causing the dogs to wander all over the track, in fact, they will sometimes trail several hundred feet off the actual track.

The effect of moisture on a track can alter the scent strength so drastically that training programs using tracks of a specific age must be altered in age to compensate for the moisture's effect on the track. Each successive track that the dog works out must smell as similar in strength as the preceding one or confusion may result. For example, a fifteen minute old track laid on a warm, windless, sunny and dry day is approximately equal to a two hour old track that has been laid on a foggy, windless, cool type of day, following a heavy rain.

Restrictive Tracking

It used to be the popular opinion that tracking dogs shouldn't be restricted when on a track. They should be tracking on a very loose (slack) line and the handler should follow the dog wherever he decided to go. This usually resulted in more dogs running off the corners or taking the handlers for a walk than

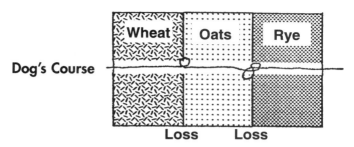

Figure 4 • **Behavior on Changes in Vegetation**

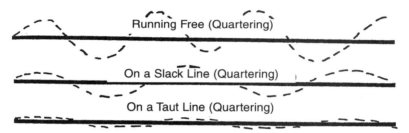

Figure 5 • **Restrictive Tracking**

actually qualifying at tracking tests. Restrictive tracking simply means that the tracking line never touches the ground between the dog and handler and is always taut from the dog's back to the handler. The dog is taught to lean into the harness and pull when he is on the track. In this manner, it doesn't matter whether you are tracking during the day when you can visually see the dog or at night in a heavy fog when you can only feel the tension on the line. Should the tension suddenly decrease, you know that the dog has stopped tracking and is possibly on a turn at that moment. When the tension increases once more in a new direction, you know he has made the turn, even though you cannot see him. I have no idea how a handler would follow or read his dog when tracking on a slack line and unable to make visual contact with his dog at night.

Should you get the dog used to tracking against this fixed amount of pressure on the line, three things will result: 1) He will be come accustomed to pulling, and it will become exceedingly difficult to pull him off a track when he is committed to it.

2) As the track becomes older, it will force him to track closer to the actual track, and his quartering will dampen out completely. 3) You will become accustomed to the dog's pulling with a certain amount of pressure when he is on the track and will be able to feel any deviation in pressure when he loses the track, indicates an article, or has detected a cross-track. You will also be able to read loss of track sooner than if you are relying on observing a visual change in behavior, allowing you to stop with the next leg of the track out in front of you, which is much easier for your dog to locate than if it is behind you. Restricting him right from the beginning of a tracking program will aid in stopping the tendency to trail if coupled with properly designed and laid out training tracks.

Restrictive Tracking

Determining Behavioral Characteristics 2

Analyzing all of the theories, stories and suggestions received at tracking tests and training sessions only confirmed my original suspicion that most were contradictory and few people involved in tracking could agree on anything. The methods I had seen and discussed were fragmentary and seemed to lack any logical form of progression. In fact, they seemed to be oriented along a "hit or miss" approach with the general consensus being that the dog had to be a "natural" to begin with, although a definition of a "natural" seemed to be a dog that could learn to track. The only logical approach at this point seemed to be to embark upon a scientific approach, conduct experiments to determine those questions that were in my mind, document them and later analyze them to see if any light could be shed upon this fascinating area of training.

The first thing was to see what would happen if I took a dog and did all of those things that were stated to be taboo. In this manner, I would be able to see first hand what the results would be. Well, to make a long story short, I did just that and ended up with a badly confused dog and file folders full of results. Analyzing the results after the fact only led to more questions, instead of any real answers. The next step was obvious. It would be necessary to work with fully trained dogs on experiments that were designed to provide answers in terms of behavior when placed in certain specific situations under controlled conditions. In this chapter I will present those experiments that seemed to produce the results that were instrumental in providing some of the most important data, which resulted in the formulation of our first tracking training program.

One question, which required answering, was whether or not a dog could successfully detect the presence of a track when the dog had to cast for the track through a field area without having been allowed any starting scent. The next diagram illustrates the track of an individual passing through a field in a straight line without making any turns whatever. The dogs were commanded to "find it" and then worked at the end of their tracking line in such a manner that they would bisect the track left by the individual who passed through the area less than a half hour before. This diagram also illustrates the dog's course when he approached the track and actually detected the track. All of the tracking dogs used in this experiment not only indicated the presence of the track, but also indicated the direction taken by their track layer. Some of the dogs would immediately take the right direction and track it to the end, while other dogs would start in the wrong direction, backtrack for up to a few yards and then turn about and start tracking it in the forward direction. This seemed to answer our question as to whether or not a dog would pick up a track when no starting scent was given to them to follow, but it also posed another question. Why was it that so many TDX hopefuls that made it to the cross tracks would pick up the cross track and track the cross track layer in the reverse direction, as well as the forward direction? Using the same basic format, the experiment was conducted once more. This time the track was bisected when the track was only one-half hour old and then another track was similarly bisected only at three hours old.

Question: Would the dogs backtrack, or would they, in fact, be

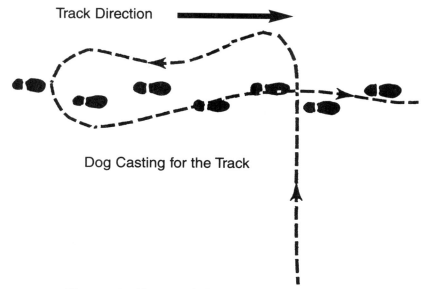

Track Direction

Dog Casting for the Track

Figure 6 • **Determining Track Direction**

capable of determining the direction taken by the track layer?

Results: When the trained dogs were introduced to the track as already described, we discovered that the dogs did not make any errors in direction more than the few yards already recorded when the track was only one-half hour old. The dogs that were introduced to the three-hour-old tracks in the same manner would sometimes backtrack and sometimes forward track. Whichever direction the dogs initially started on, after bisecting the track, was the direction they continued in.

Conclusions:
1. There is no doubt that the trained tracking dogs (trained to forward track) could tell the direction taken by a track layer within a few yards of investigation, provided the track was less than one-half hour old.

2. The same trained tracking dogs could not tell the direction taken by the track layer if the track was three

hours old.
3. There must be a substantial difference between the scent of a track one-half hour old and a track three hours old.

To ensure that this phenomenon was not a result of wind direction, we repeated the experiments under four differing wind conditions. The tracks were laid first with the track layer going into the wind; secondly, with the track layer going with the wind; and thirdly, with a crosswind blowing from the track layer's right and then blowing from his left. The dogs exhibited the same tendencies. They did not make any errors on the fresh tracks, but would track the older tracks in the first direction they started in, whether it was backtracking or forward tracking.

Previous experimentation had revealed the possibility that a tracking dog could not tell who had laid an old track of more than two hours in age. These results affirmed the necessity of additional experiments to determine whether or not the dogs were, in fact, following the scent of an individual, or were they capable of following a track left by a track layer other than a human being. The decision was made to try the dogs on a track that would bear no body odor whatever to see if the dogs would, in fact, still be capable of following it. A weighted tire rim was placed in the middle of a field area at one end of the field and long ropes were attached to it that could reach either end of the narrow field. After three weeks in the elements, the experiment was ready to be attempted. Two individuals were assigned to take the ends of the rope at the sides of the field and they dragged the tire rim across the field to the other side. Thirty minutes later the dog was cast across the field in such a manner that he would bisect the track left by the tire rim as we had done in the previous detailed experiment. When the dog reached the track, he indicated discovery of the track and proceeded to track the rim across the field. This verified, in my mind, that the tracking dog would readily track down a scent that bore no resemblance to human odor whatever. This scent I have already defined in the previous chapter as "track scent."

Now I was faced with another question. What was there about the age of a track that resulted in the dog's obvious difficulty in determining the direction of the track after a long period of time? Was it possible that the individual's body odor made it possible for the dog to determine the direction of the track, and was it also possible that the individual's body odor was no longer present after a long period of time? This could answer the question of older tracks. These problems required additional experimentation before we could arrive at any concrete conclusions.

Should our theory be correct, the tracking dogs should be able to tell the difference between two track layers if the tracks were fresh and be unable to distinguish between two different track layers if the tracks were very old. On this basis using an "X" pattern, the first series I conducted had one track layer start at one corner of a field while another track layer started from another corner of the same field, both meeting in the center of the field and executing a right angle turn. Thirty minutes later the tracking dogs were started on the track of one of the track layers.

Question: Would the tracking dog be able to discern the difference between the two track layers when he arrived at the center of the "X" pattern or would he simply continue onto the the track of the other track layer?

Results: In every case, the dogs indicated loss of track when arriving at the center of the "X" pattern and after a short period of searching for the new direction of the track discovered and followed it to its conclusion.

Conclusion: When employed on a relatively fresh track, the dogs can, in fact, distinguish between two different track layers and will not be confused by the presence of another track.

Question: Would the tracking dog be capable of discerning the difference between the two track layers when arriving at the center of the "X" pattern of a three-hour-old track, or would he simply continue onto the track of the second track layer?

Results: When the dogs were started on the track of one track layer and arrived at the center of the "X" pattern, they would sometimes indicate a loss of track and would then continue on

Figure 7 • Track layers of Equal Weight at Three Hours

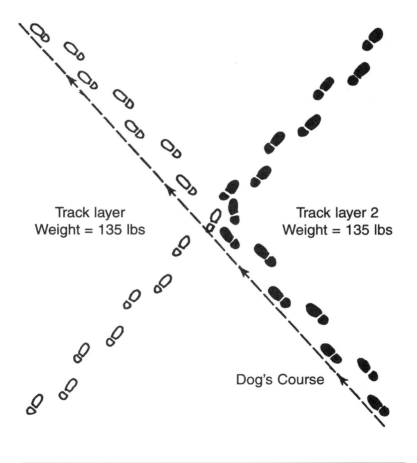

Track layer
Weight = 135 lbs

Track layer 2
Weight = 135 lbs

Dog's Course

Tracking Dog Theory & Methods

to the conclusion of the correct track. Sometimes they would carry on to follow the track of the second track layer with no indication whatever of having discerned any difference between the two tracks.

Figure 8 • **Track layers of Differing Weight at Three Hours**

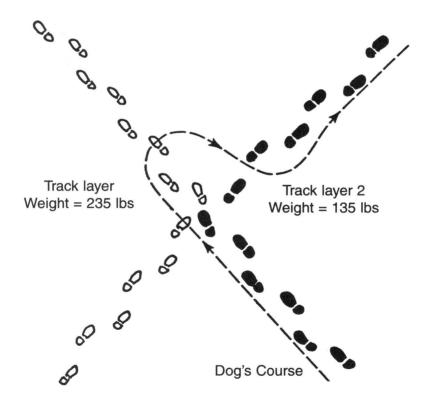

Track layer
Weight = 235 lbs

Track layer 2
Weight = 135 lbs

Dog's Course

Conclusion: Those track which resulted in the dog's accurately discerning the difference between the two track layers were separated from those where the dogs had failed to discern any difference between the two track layers and analyzed for differences that might account for the discrepancy. Here it was noted that the tracks, which resulted in errors on the part of the dogs, had one thing in common, the respective weights of the persons laying the two tracks were almost identical, while those tracks that resulted in no errors on the part of the dogs had track layers of considerable weight difference.

This series of experiments seemed to point toward the possibility that the tracking dogs were following scent strength, rather than the body odor of the individual track layers. This called for a repeat of the same "X" pattern experiments, only with track layers of comparable weights in one case and substantially differing weights in another case.

Question: Could the tracking dogs distinguish between the scents of two track layers on a fresh track when the respective weights of the track layers were (1) substantially different, (2) identical?

Results: The dogs made no error on the "X" pattern when the track was fresh, regardless of the weight of the two track layers.

Conclusion: Tracking dogs could discern the difference between two tracks of identical age regardless of the weight of the track layers when the tracks they were following were relatively fresh.

Question: Could the tracking dogs distinguish between the scents of two track layers on a three-hour-old track when the respective weights of the two track layers were (1) substantially different, (2) identical?

Results: The tracking dogs made no error on the "X" pattern when the tracks were aged and the weights of the two track layers were substantially different, but when the weights of the two track layers were identical, the tracking dogs gave no indication whatever of having lost the track when arriving at the center of the "X" pattern, and they continued onto the track of the second track layer without even breaking stride.

Conclusion: It was obvious that the tracking dogs were, in fact, following the relative scent strength of the track and no body odor when on aged tracks, but were following body odor, as well as track scent on the fresh tracks. The dogs were discriminating between the two different track layers by "scent discrimination" on fresh tracks, but discriminating between the two track layers on the aged tracks by "scent strength discrimination." When the two track layers were of identical weights, there was no difference to discriminate between; therefore, the dogs made the error. In actuality, the dogs had not made an error; they believed the track of the second person to be the same as the first when the weights were identical.

From these experiments and others we had conducted, it was apparent that the dogs were following the body odor, plus track scent, during their initial training when the tracks were fresh. At some point in time, the scent, which the tracking dogs were following had to change to track scent exclusively, totally devoid of body odor. When this transition took place was, as yet, unknown, and its relative importance in training dogs to track was, still an unknown quantity. In researching the earlier records made when attending tracking tests, as well as those gathered in conversations with the "old-timers" in tracking, certain statements began to take on great importance.

Many handlers had mentioned to me that they had dogs that tracked beautifully on 15 to 20 minute tracks, yet the same dogs could not perform with reliability on an hour old track. Dogs that drew the first track in the morning at one tracking test would perform well, yet at another test, when they drew one of the later tracks that was run near noon, the dogs wouldn't even start. Practically every handler I met at tracking test hoped for one of the first tracks because they seemed to have more confidence in passing it than a later track which they tended to dread.

The first several dogs that went through our newly formulated tracking program experienced the same sort of difficulty when we approached the 30 to 60 minute mark of the aging of the tracks. Putting all of this information together prompted me to theorize on what might be causing this phenomenon to affect the performance of so many apparently good dogs. I already knew that the first odor to diminish to zero was the individual's body odor on a track while the track scent itself would remain for great periods of time. Was it possible that the dogs learned to follow body odor during the beginning stages of their training and then at some point in time this body odor would continue to diminish until the track scent was stronger than the body odor? This could result in tracking dogs in training to suddenly discover that the scent they are supposed to be following is no longer detectable and they would indicate a loss of track and be unable to find it again. When dogs that are trained to follow this body odor are put on a track that has no body odor remaining, then they would be lost before they even started, which could account for the problems I had heard and seen.

Researching all of the recorded data I had maintained enabled me to construct a chart that shows the behavior of body odor and track scent, as believe it to be. This drew my attention to the moment in time that I refer to as "the hump." This "hump" theory has contributed greatly to the modification of my original tracking training program and enabled me to produce the 100% record that my tracking classes have had over the past several years.

Examination of the "Time Versus Scent Strength" chart shows that at the moment the track is laid, both scents are at their strongest, but the stronger or more perceptible scent at that first moment in time is the body odor of the person laying the track. The question of body odor disappearing completely after such a short period of time was doubted by most tracking enthusiasts of the day, regardless of the experiment results. It wasn't until I caught myself, along with most other handlers of Utility dogs, doing a simple, inconsequential thing every day that I had the chart reaffirmed. When attempting to eliminate the handler's own odor from those articles he had just used, most handlers simply left them outside to "aid" out before mixing them in with all of the other articles. The scent imparted to the articles came directly from the skin of the handler and should the handler be sweating heavily at the time they were to be used, they received a much heavier dosage of body odor than would the footprint of a human being stepping onto a vegetated area. After a couple of hours in a hot sun with lots of air circulation, the articles had lost sufficient body odor to make it impossible for most dogs to detect which article had been touched.

A simple experiment was devised to see how long body odor would be retained by an article when left to air in the elements of a hot, windy day. The articles used were handled in different ways. Some were simply placed upon the hand of the handler for one minute. Some were pressed once between the open palms. Some were rubbed lightly and others were spat upon and rubbed vigorously. The dogs used for this experiment were dogs that had proven their proficiency at scent discrimination and had already acquired the Utility Dog titles. The articles that were scented were placed in the open air under conditions of high heat and wind for one hour before the dogs were asked to retrieve the articles that had been scented. The only article they would detect correctly at all was the one that had been spat upon and rubbed vigorously and most of the dogs missed even that one. These trained dogs missed all of the other articles.

This confirmed my belief that the body odor of a track layer would either completely disappear or be reduced to an indiscernible quantity after a short period of time when exposed to conditions that enhanced evaporation. Therefore, I concluded, the chart's description of body odor disappearing first before the track scent itself was substantially correct. The only undetermined detail was — when did this actually occur when weather conditions, conditions of vegetation, etc. were constantly changing? Examination of this chart also showed that there would be one moment in time when the two scents, the body odor and the track scent, would be equal in strength, but different in scent content. This moment in time was also appearing to be around that time when so many dogs were experiencing difficulty in their tracking.

Dogs that are trained to track are normally trained to follow a fresh track for a considerable period of time before tracks are aged to any degree. Was it possible that the novice tracking dog trained to follow body odor over a long period of time would become confused when he could no longer detect this body odor? The track scent itself would probably appear to the dog as something that was different, not the scent he was supposed to find, resulting in a dog that could no longer function because the scent he was to follow was nowhere to be found. This could, in fact, answer why so many dogs were excellent trackers on fresh tracks laid early in the morning, but couldn't follow a track laid later during the day when evaporation was increased. This moment in time had to be overcome and the dogs taught that the track scent, even though different from the body odor they were accustomed to follow also led to the desired article at the end of the track. This moment in time represented a hurdle, or "hump," which the dogs had to surmount before they could function efficiently as tracking dogs on the more aged tracks.

By incorporating this finding into my tracking training program, as described in chapter 4, under training methods, I discovered that there were many variables affecting the moment in time when the hump would occur. I was unable to pinpoint the exact time when this phenomenon would occur, but by evolving the table shown here, I could come reasonably close to pinpointing this moment in time. Once the approximate time span where the hump would occur was determined, it was a simple matter of obtaining the exact time of occurrence for that particular time of day, as described in chapter 4 under the training methods used to surmount this hump. In order to accomplish this, I discovered that certain variables played the greatest role in affecting the hump and simply allocated a numerical system to each, based upon the rate at which evaporation would occur as follows:

Variable	Condition of Variable	Evaporation Rate	Number allocated
Wind	None	Low	3
	Medium Velocity	Medium	2
	High Velocity	Fast	1

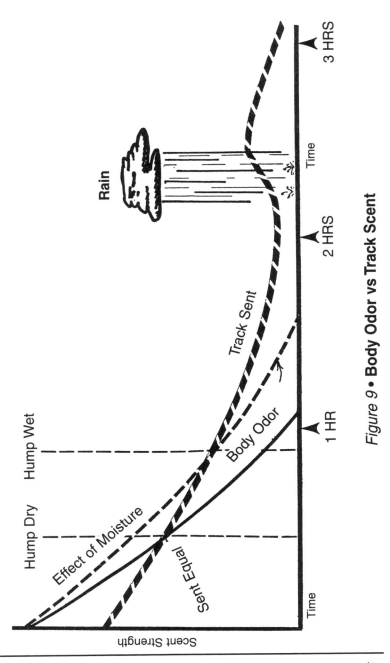

Figure 9 • **Body Odor vs Track Scent**

The higher the number allocated meant that evaporation time was the longest. In other words, the longer it should take for body odor to dissipate. On this basis, I formulated the table shown here.

Wind	Low	Med	High
Temp.	Low	Med	High
Humidity	High	Med	Low
Veg.	Lush	Med	Sparse
Weather	Overcast	Dull Sun	Bright
Time	Morning	Evening	Afternoon
Number	3	2	1
Hump	90 Min.	60 Min.	30 Min.
Factor	X5	X5	X5
Total	18	12	6

In the first case of the table addition of the number allocations (3+3+3+3+3+3) gave us a total of 18 points and the hump was very close to 90 minutes. In the last case shown on the table where each variable was equated with a numerical rating of 1, the addition of each variable rating totaled 6 and the hump occurred very close to 30 minutes. Closer examination of these consistent findings showed a definite relationship existing between the two totals and the actual occurrence of the hump. In both cases, if the hump in minutes were divided by a factor of 5, I would arrive at the total of the numerical allocations for each variable. This meant that if we were to total the numerical allocations of each variable and multiply them by 5, it would give me a result that was very close to where I would actually find the hump.

I have no doubt that research into this phenomenon will produce a far more accurate method of determining the moment in time when the hump actually occurs. My method will produce inaccuracies of as much as 10 minutes on a predicted hump occurring around the 30 minute mark and as much as 30 minutes on a prediction of 90 minutes, but it will place the hump at a point in time that is accurate enough for me to determine the exact moment when it occurs by using the following process in a tracking class.

Having predicted the hump occurring at 30 minutes, tracks will be laid out for a class of six dogs in sets of two. The first dog will track a thirty-minute-old track while watched closely to see if he experiences any difficulty throughout the track. Should he have difficulty at about the third leg of his track, then the handler must literally lead the dog the rest of the way while encouraging him to "find it." If the dog picks up again and completes the track on his own, he is then taken immediately to his second track, which is about ten minutes older than the first and should present him with even greater difficulty. The dog will not have any difficulty with this older track if he has resumed tracking on the previous track on his own and the age of each successive track during his training can now be increased in leaps and bounds.

Should the first dog experience no difficulty on this first track of 30 minutes, then I know the hump is at a point in time further on, so the next dog will be put on a track that is 35 minutes old. Each successive track is increased in age by 5 minutes until the first dog experiences difficulty and the hump is found. Now we know how old to age the tracks in order to force the dog into problems on the track, lead him with great encouragement to follow the new track scent, and then place him on a 10 minute older track to verify that he is now following the track scent itself.

One tracking class, in particular, comes to mind when we predicted the time of occurrence of the hump and the first dog experienced difficulty on the last leg of a track that had three turns and four legs. Since it was in the middle of a summer morning, and the sun was rising, as well as the temperature, I anticipated that each of the remaining five dogs should experience difficulty sooner on the track. Sure enough, the next dog had difficulty when he arrived at the last turn and could not detect the last leg of the track and was led to its conclusion. The third dog had his trouble half way down the third leg, the fourth dog had trouble half way down the second leg, the fifth dog had problems in locating the track on the first turn and the sixth dog couldn't even get away from the starting flag. Each of these dogs ended up resuming the track only after being led part way with great encouragement and none had any problem with their second track, which was 10 minutes older than the first, and all dogs went on to obtain their TD titles.

It has been my experience that quite often the handlers will surmount this hump on their own when training their dogs during the week, as long as they lead their dog with great encouragement along the remainder of the track. I have no doubt that some dogs will overcome this problem on their own by chance, especially if this hump occurs just before they arrive at the article, which reinforces the dogs' belief that this new scent did, in fact, lead to the article they were after.

During my experimentations and the initial training program operation, I discovered that the novice tracking dog could follow a track much easier if the track layer had walked over the same place more than once, and I wondered just how much would the scent strength of the track be affected by this repeated walking over the same track. I had assumed that perhaps it would result in increasing the track scent by twofold if a person walked over the same track twice. In order to determine this, I decided to use fully trained dogs on a single laid track, as opposed to a double laid track. The dogs had no difficulty following either track when they were up to three hours old, but from that point in time, the single laid track began to pose a real problem for the dogs. Not so the double laid track. I extended the age of the tracks to eight hours, which resulted in the dogs' being unable to pick up the single laid track at all. They had no difficulty whatever with the double laid track. This seemed to me as if the track scent had been increased by more than double, perhaps it increases by the square. I never had the opportunity to continue on with the experiment. However, it did tell me that using a double laid track would make it much easier for a dog in training to detect the presence of a track. This characteristic I found accelerated the dogs' learning how to handle turns, as described in chapter 4 under training methods.

These experiments, plus countless others, provided me with the necessary information to formulate a logical, effective training program which, with very slight modifications, has been our standby in producing extraordinary results with all breeds of dogs. They still do not tell us how a dog uses his nose to locate a particular odor, nor do they give us a measure of the dog's olfactory capability. They simply show us what kinds of behavior we can expect when the dog is confronted with certain situations that he will find in tracking. By utilizing these characteristics in a training program, we can more effectively present the training to a dog. This program is more conducive to his learning and will give us a better understanding of his problems and the types of behavior he will exhibit when confronted with these problems.

Sherry, English Cocker Spaniel, first dog to earn all Canadian and American Obedience and Tracking Titles, as well as being a breed champion in both countries.

Tracking
Training
Essentials 3

Starting into a tracking training program requires that the prospective handler plan ahead and obtain the necessary equipment ahead of time. The amount of time that the handler is going to have to put in training his dog in tracking is no more than the time required by the average person to train a dog in novice obedience work. About one hour a day should suffice in order to complete this program. The handler will discover that while he has to work very hard during that hour, the dog is only working for about fifteen minutes each day. Before the actual training begins, the handler should be familiar with the tools he is going to work with and how to use them. This chapter deals specifically with these things: the equipment that is required, the essentials of how to use the equipment, track laying and the basic fundamentals of handling when training a dog in restrictive tracking. First the equipment.

Equipment
1. A non-restrictive tracking harness
2. A fifty foot long tracking line that is weatherproof

---

3. Six leather articles and two non-leather articles
4. Eight tracking stakes with easily observed flagging
5. Rain gear – rubber boots, pants and a jacket
   with a hood that is waterproof
6. Mosquito repellent
7. Clipboard, paper (for map making) and a waterproof marker
8. Container for water, drinking water from
   handler's locale and a dish
9. One dog in good health

The last item mentioned is the most important item on the list
and is the one item we'll examine first.

Breeds Capable of Tracking

In every breed of dog you'll find animals capable of
tracking. As a matter of fact, I have not yet come across a breed
of dog that could not learn to track. In the tracking training programs that I conduct, almost every group has had representa-
tives entered in the training program that have acquired their
tracking title. The larger breeds have less trouble with the heavily overgrown areas filled with underbrush and seem to handle
the stamina requirements of the long TDX tracks with less
fatigue, but learning to track is not the sole domain of any single group or groups of dogs.

In my classes I have had everything from ten-year-old near-
ly blind Toy Poodles to the gigantic Irish Wolfhound. Some of
the breeds who have acquired their Tracking Dog Excellent
titles have been English Cocker Spaniels, Toy Poodles, Shetland
Sheepdogs, German Shepherd dogs and Bouvier Des Flanders.
One handler who attended a tracking symposium I gave went
home armed with the tracking program detailed in the Trainer's
Handbook at the end of this book and within a few months
earned a Canadian and American T.D. title on her Maltese
Terrier, a four and a half pound tracking dynamo. It is my
contention that any dog that can walk, has a nose, breathes and
is reasonably responsive to the handler can be taught to track.
This isn't to say that I believe all breeds will have the same

capability when it comes to tracking, for this hasn't been the case. Some breeds of dogs seem to have a greater capacity for this type of training, while some breeds seem to reach their olfactory limitations sooner than other breeds. For example, all four-legged animals have the ability to run, but some species have the capability to run faster or further than other species.

Many times I have been asked whether the Bloodhound is the best tracking dog, or is it another breed? I honestly cannot answer this question since I have never seen any sort of controlled competition between breeds of dogs to determine this point. Should one go by the records maintained by Kennel Clubs on the results of licensed tracking tests, you'd probably find that more German Shepherd dogs acquire their titles than any other single breed, but this is probably due to the fact that there are more German Shepherd dogs entered in tracking tests than any other breed. From my own experience, I would have to say that those dogs from the working group, once trained, are the more proficient tracking dogs and the sporting group would rank second. However, you do find individual dogs of a certain breed may be more proficient than another dog of another breed due to the differences in temperament, tractability and intelligence.

More important than the breed of dog is the selection of a dog as a candidate for a tracking program that will, in fact, learn easily and have the capability.

Selection of Dogs for Tracking

All dogs have noses; their noses have olfactory systems. Therefore, all dogs have the ability to smell. Some dogs have better noses than other dogs, but this you'll not discover until the dog is trained in tracking and their limitations are reached. This simply means that their scenting ability is not a criterion for their possible selection as a candidate for tracking training. Not all dogs are natural retrievers, many of them have to be taught to retrieve and some dogs will not even pursue a ball when thrown. Past experience has taught me that the dog possessing a compulsive, natural instinct for retrieving is more easily trained to track than the dog that is not a natural retriever.

Mr. Feather, 4 lb. Maltese Terrier
Canadian and American TD

Teil, Shetland Sheepdog
Canadian TDX and American TD

Kimo, Bouvier Des Flandres
Canadian TD

Mac, Irish Wolfhound
Canadian and American TD

This criterion for selection of a dog for tracking training doesn't mean that the non-retrieving dog will be unable to learn tracking, nor does it mean that the best tracking dogs are natural retrievers. One dog in particular comes to mind that would not retrieve and, although it took a little longer to teach this dog tracking, it became the best tracking dog I have ever encountered. I am simply saying that the natural retriever is easier to teach tracking from the standpoint of "work by the handler."

The more stable dogs, that are not hyperactive, with an attention span that is long, make the better trackers when the track becomes longer, older and distractions are present when the dog is on a track. The more tractable (responsive to the handler) the dog is, the easier it is to train in tracking. Dogs that are kennel dogs and have not had the opportunity to establish a rapport with the handler have difficulties in learning to track, while those dogs that have established this rapport are the easiest to train.

The ideal candidate for tracking training is a dog that seems to walk around with a lazy expression as if he were saying "DUH" all the time and possesses such a natural compulsive instinct to retrieve that even though half asleep on the floor, cannot contain himself when a ball rolls past him, and who has a strong rapport with his handler. This type of dog has a strong, courageous temperament and is not hyperactive.

Over the past years, I have noticed that young puppies (over three months) that have not received any training in competitive obedience learn to track much quicker than dogs that have undergone a great deal of competitive training. This fact may be due to the nature of the training itself. Those dogs that have been compulsively trained in obedience are the ones that have problems when in tracking training, while those dogs that have been trained to an equal level or higher in obedience with inductive training methods exhibit none of these problems. I believe that this group of dogs that is trained with too much compulsion has learned to dislike training itself and has lost the desire to play in a training situation. Tracking training employs this "game" feature to a large extent. The best age to start a dog into tracking training appears to be between four and six months of age.

Scent discrimination training, as found in the Utility class of obedience, has no bearing whatever as an asset or liability when it comes to tracking training. Contrary to the belief of many novices in training, the tendency of a dog to constantly sniff the ground, floors or objects is not an indication that the dog will do well in tracking.

All breeds of dogs can be taught to track, whether they are natural retrievers or have no retrieving instincts at all. Selection of a dog specifically for tracking should be made from the working or sporting group with consideration for certain physical attributes. Long coats have the tendency to pick up more burrs, ice balls, and mud than dogs with short or medium coats. Heavy coats are a liability when tracking long distances in hot, sunny weather, contributing to fatigue. The medium or large breeds can surmount obstacles, such as large ditches, fences and heavy underbrush more easily than the smaller breeds.

The question has been asked of me many times whether the "country dog" or the "city dog" makes the best tracking dogs. The assumption here is that the country, or farm dog, has already learned to use his nose around the farm, while the city dog has never really had the opportunity to use his to any great extent. I would have to agree with the assumption that the country dog, in all probability, has learned to use his nose, but not to follow the track of a stranger on command. As a matter of experience, I have noticed that the farm dog has learned what raccoons are, as well as what field mice, game birds, and other non-desirable attractions are. This usually presents us with a problem in correcting the dog's natural instinct to pursue these unwanted prizes, which the city dog has never learned about. The city dog, on the other hand, has not formed the same undesirable behavior and has probably learned to verify things with his nose or with his eyes. This dog usually learns as quickly as the farm dog, but without the same problematic behavior.

The Non-Restrictive Harness

There are many different types of harnesses on the market today, but most of them are not suited to restrictive tracking.

The best harness should not have any restriction on the dog's shoulders when he is moving. The typical walking harness, available at most pet shops, has this shoulder strap which interferes with the dog's movement when he is leaning into the harness on a taut line. This results in discomfort to the dog, and after a short period of time, he will stop his pulling to avoid this discomfort. The ideal harness depicted in the photograph should be lightweight, made of leather, nylon or canvas and be adjustable around his neck and rib cage, so that it will fit him like a glove. The backstrap and the belly strap should be fixed permanently to the straps that encircle his rib cage so that the harness will not rotate around him when pressure is applied by the line from the side. At the rear of the backstrap there is a "D" ring where the line can be attached when working the dog.

The Tracking Line

The tracking line I prefer for restrictive tracking is the lightweight, pliable 1/4" diameter nylon. The dog can easily pull this type of line through underbrush without snagging, and it is very easy to handle on turns or when maintaining tautness on the straightaway. Rain will not soak into it, increasing its weight nor will the wind start it flapping furiously. A snap should be connected to one end, a small knot tied at the minimum length and a large knot tied at the thirty-foot mark. The maximum length, dictated by the rules of the testing organization, should be observed, for it will differ considerably. When tracking in the open fields, the thirty-foot knot is where the handler should work, and when moving into heavy cover, the handler should move closer to the dog, but not any closer than the minimum length knot. During the training of the handler and dog, I recommend a 50-yard line that can later be reduced to conform to existing rules.

Articles

Six of the articles should be leather, but different in appearance. These may be obtained at any shoemaker or saddlery as scrap pieces. You can also use gloves, wallets, key cases, small shoes, belts or billfolds. Always carry one of these articles with

Non-Restrictive Tracking Harness

you when your dog is tracking just in case the dog does get lost, you have to terminate the track for some reason or, Lord forbid, someone has passed that way before you put the dog on the track and has taken the article with him. In one case, when I was following behind a Shetland Sheepdog working out a TDX track that I had laid three hours before, we discovered that there was no article at the end of the track where I had left it. The handler terminated the track by throwing out the article she was carrying just as a farmer came into view. He asked what we were looking for and when I answered, "You might not believe this, but it's an old shoe," he stated rather matter of factly, "Oh, that old shoe. I picked it up and took it back to the house for my dog to play with." It is always wise to carry this one article so that you can throw it out onto the track when you terminate a track unsuccessfully. In this manner, the dog is always successful in his efforts.

Tracking Stakes

In the early stages of training, you must know where the start of your track is, which direction the track goes in, exactly where each turn is, and where the article is supposed to be. To accomplish this, you'll need at least eight stakes, about four feet in length, lightweight so that you can carry them into the field with you, and with some sort of flagging on top that you can see from a couple of hundred yards distance. One end should be sharpened to permit easy insertion into the ground and the stake itself should be painted white for easy identification at a distance. I find that 3/8" dowel makes an ideal type of stake or, if not available, corner molding is next best.

Additional Equipment

Weather should not be a criteria for tracking because you'll find tracking tests held in all sorts of weather, and whoever heard of a person getting lost only on sunny days? In order to have a dog that will function properly under adverse weather conditions, you must train him under these conditions, as well as when it is comfortable for you, the handler. A good waterproof suit of clothing is a must when tracking in the rain, and you'll find that heavy dew settling on the fields early in the morning can result in your getting soaked up to the waist if you do not have waterproof pants to protect you. I have found that dogs will track equally well, whether the track layer wears rubber or leather footwear, so in order to protect yourself from sloshing around all morning in wet socks, wear rubber boots.

Equipment for Tracking Training

Should your rain gear not have a hood with it, you may discover, to your chagrin, that the rain will run off your head, down your neck, and under the waterproof jacket you are wearing. The pants should fit over top of the rubber boots to prevent water from running down the pant legs into your boots.

Mosquitoes can be a plague, especially when tracking in a swampy sort of an area and can be just as much a discomfort to the handler as to the dog. Liberal spraying of repellent will increase the comfort of both handler and dog when tracking through mosquito territory. Spraying repellent on the dog may not prevent heartworm, but it will reduce the number of mosquito bites, and thus reduce the chances of your dog getting this parasite.

The drinking water from your locale is for dog and handler at the end of a track when the dog and handler will be tired and thirsty. Always tend to your dog's needs immediately upon concluding a track. Under adverse weather conditions, you'll discover that pencils do not write very well on wet paper when mapmaking, and water soluble pens will run all over the wet paper, making the map indiscernible a few minutes later, so use a waterproof marker when making maps of the tracks. Very few track layers, even veterans, can tell exactly where the track is after a period of time has expired since laying the track. Since it is critically important to know exactly where the track is at all times during training, it is much easier to tell where the track is if a map is made of the track when it is laid.

Tracking Training Areas

The type of area that should be selected as a starting area for tracking training should be as conducive to the dog's learning as possible with as few obstacles in it as possible that might discourage the dog. Ideally, it should be heavily vegetated with reasonably short grass. The ideal height of grass should be approximately up to your dog's pastern or slightly higher. Once the program is well underway, other types of vegetation should be used, such as stubble fields, wheat, rye or other grain fields and pasture land that has a liberal sprinkling of manure. Great care should be exercised when tracking in stubble fields with a constant surveillance of the dog's legs and underbelly. Should you attempt to walk through a stubble field wearing a pair of shorts and low shoes, you'll painfully notice that the sharp stubble will badly scratch your legs. This type of irritation will cause many dogs to start chewing at themselves, causing eczema to break out. Should this chewing tendency appear, it is wise to stay out of stubble fields for some time. The short vegetation will enable you to see exactly what your dog is doing and give you the opportunity to practice your lead handling before entering rough terrain. When the dog is tracking well, he should be introduced to rough cover, underbrush and treed areas where both handler and dog can gain experience.

Track Laying

The number of tools you have to work with when creating a tracking dog are few in number, the most important being the track itself. No matter how well-designed beforehand, the track is useless if improperly laid or if the handler is unaware of its

---

precise location. Should your dog get into trouble in the middle of a track, it is a must to know exactly where the track is in order to restart him. Imagine the dog's confusion if you are attempting to restart him where there is no track. All the encouragement in the world won't help should the sought after track be several yards away from where the dog is searching, and it doesn't take very much of this situation to result in a dog that simply quits. A track layer who doesn't know where his track is within a few inches is more of a liability than an asset. It is wise to commence tracking training with another student of tracking so that each of you will recognize the importance of a well laid track.

I have met very few people that could walk in a straight line when out in an open field area. The majority have the tendency to walk in an arc or curve to their right. One student of mine had this tendency so bad that after going only one hundred yards, supposedly in a straight line, she found herself almost 100 yards to the right of her intended destination. Another problem that contributes to the track layer's inability to locate his track with precision is the changing light that results from the sun changing its position in the sky with time, creating a whole new set of shadows and appearances of the field. This makes the field look completely different to the track layer after a period of time has elapsed.

Should a dog experience difficulty while tracking, either on a straightaway or a turn, I expect the track layer to be able to walk up to where the track or turn is and place a stake in the ground exactly where the track or turn is supposed to be so that the dog can be restarted exactly where the track is known to be. This does not mean within a couple of feet of the track, but exactly where the track is. In order to do this, the track layer must know beforehand how to lay a track, how to walk in a straight line and how to make an accurate map of his track, using natural markers that he will include in his map. This capability is not natural, but is the result of training and experience.

In order to fully appreciate the difficulty involved with laying a track and recalling exactly where the track actually is, I have my student tracking trainees lay out a simple track which possesses one turn with each leg about 100 yards in length and use no marking stakes whatever. At the end of the track I have them deposit a penny and return along their same footsteps. One hour later I have these same students attempt to retrace their steps and pick up the penny. If they cannot find the penny, I let them stay out in the field looking for it for about thirty minutes. Upon their return (usually without the penny), I point out the fact that, should a dog lose the track at that same point where the penny should have been, they would have been unable to tell me exactly where the track was, and I would have had to terminate the track by throwing out an article for the dog to find. I believe this little exercise is one that all prospective students of tracking should attempt in order to appreciate the difficulty of precise track laying.

When laying a track at the start of a tracking program, there are no turns involved. The single leg must be laid in a straight line and marked in such a manner that the handler knows at all times where the track actually is. To start the track, you place the first stake in the ground on your left side and trample down an area of about one square yard beside the stake. This trampled down area is where the dog will be started and the handler will always know that it is to the right of the starting stake, even if he has not seen you lay the track. Select two (not one) objects in the distance that are a considerable distance apart (but in line with each other) and begin to walk toward these two objects while keeping them in line with each other. You should be able to line these two objects up much as you would the front and far sights of a rifle. Should you move even a single pace off your intended route, you'll immediately notice a change in their perspective and they will not line up. Your steps should be normal, no scraping of the feet, and after ten paces (thirty paces once the dog is trained), place a second stake in the ground, also on your left side. This stake will tell the handler which direction you have taken and he'll know you passed the stake to the right of it. Continue to walk in a straight line while maintaining the perspective you have started with until you reach the conclusion of the track. At the end of the track, drop the article directly on the track, take another step past the article and place a third stake in the ground immediately in front of you. This will tell the handler not only where you went, but also where the article is. At the conclusion of any track, regardless of how many turns or articles there are on the track, you should take an additional fifteen to twenty-five paces past the last article before you turn to leave the field. In this manner, you'll have laid a track that the handler knows is correct, and one that will enable you to locate the track by lining up the same two objects at any point on the track should the dog have to be restarted.

I cannot stress enough the actual method of placing the article to be found by the dog, whether in a training situation or when laying a track at a tracking test. The track layer must ensure that the article bears some of his scent before he places it on a track. It is suggested that he carry the article against his skin under his arm or armpit while laying a track. At the conclusion of a track, when in a training situation, he should place it on the ground in front of him and step on it as he passes over it to ensure that it is, in fact, on the track.

I have witnessed a licensed tracking test where an excellent tracking performance was given by a young German Shepherd that never circled a single turn. He simply executed a right or left turn precisely where the turns were and was disqualified when he failed to indicate the glove. Where the glove was supposed to be was where the dog executed another perfect turn to follow the track layer out of the field, resulting in the judge's whistle. Later investigation showed that the track layer, a novice who had no experience with tracking dogs, had come to a halt at that vital point, thrown the glove downwind and made a 90 degree turn to leave the track. Needless to say, even the best tracking dog in the world could not have located the glove if he had stayed right on the track. Perhaps a not-so-well-trained dog could have done so had he overshot the turn and accidentally run across the glove.

When the student track layer is laying these single leg tracks that have no turns in them, he should start looking ahead about forty to fifty paces before the designated end of the track. He should try to pick out a natural marker present in the field at approximately the end of the track he's laying, such as a partic-

ular weed, stump, change in coloration of the vegetation or anything that makes the point of concluding the track look different
from the remainder of the track. This will enable him to pick
out the conclusion of a track or a turn in the track from forty to
fifty yards behind the dog when he is following the dog/handler
team. Should the dog or handler go past this point, he will be
able to spot it the very moment the dog arrives at the designated
point, even when there are no stakes to mark these points. These
natural markers must be included on any map the track layer is
making when there are no stakes left in the ground to mark
these points later on in the track training program.

When the first turns are to be included in the tracking program of any dog, the turns are to be marked by stakes in the following manner. Arriving at the point where a turn is to be made,
the track layer should come to a halt and, without moving his
feet, place a stake in the ground on the opposite side of the
direction he is going to take from the corner. If he is going to
make a left turn, the stake should be placed in the ground about
arm's length distance to the track layer's right. (See Figure 10.)
Once the stake is in the ground, the track layer should execute a
90 degree turn away from the stake and lay the second leg in
the same manner as I have described for the first leg. If the
track has to be triple laid, the track layer simply has to make an
about turn and head directly toward the stake he has placed in
the ground to identify the turn. Any additional turns are to be
made in the same manner when identifying stakes are used. The
handler will know when he sees a turn coming up to look for
the next turn stake and will know that the track leads away from
this identifying stake toward the next stake. (Refer to the stake
positioning in Figure 10.)

By the time that all stakes are to come down, the track layer
will have become accustomed to looking for natural markers in
the field about forty to fifty yards before a turn is to be made.
The schedule outlining the distances of each leg in the next
chapter on training methods should be used as a guide rather
than a law. Should the schedule call for a leg distance of one
hundred yards, the track layer should start looking for a natural
marker in the field at about the fifty yard mark. If the track

layer selects a natural marker, which proves to be at the one hundred twelve yard mark, then that is the point where he should make his turn. This means that he will be able to follow behind the dog tracking and tell from a considerable distance behind when the dog arrives at the turn and when the handler arrives at the turn. Should the dog overshoot the turn by a distance greater than the length of the lead, he will be able to call the handler back to the exact position of the turn to restart his dog.

When you select an object(s) to line up with when laying the track, make sure the object(s) are fixed and cannot move. During a tracking fun match held several years ago, a track layer was at a loss when the dog made its turn at a point where he was sure there was no turn. While the dog continued on the track, I asked the track layer why he was so sure that there was no track where the dog was obviously tracking well. The track layer explained that he had made his turn when he was even with a parked car that was only a short distance from the turn. Investigation later, after the dog completed its track successfully, showed that the driver of the car had returned to his car after the track had been laid to move the vehicle further back so that it wouldn't present a distraction to the dog that was to follow that track. Needless to say, the track layer never made that mistake again.

Care must be exercised by the track layer to ensure that all of his legs are, in fact, straight even once the stakes are no longer used to mark the turns. Should he arrive at a burr bush, swamp hole, irrigation ditch or other obstacle which the dog is physically capable of handling, he should continue through it so that the novice handler will have the opportunity to handle the dog on the track which he knows proceeds in a straight line. Once the dog and handler are experienced and ready for competition, the track layer need not be so concerned about perfectly straight legs in the track or where he actually makes his turns, so long as he knows at all times exactly where the track and turns are located.

The use of novice track layers that have never laid a track before should be limited to those individuals who have received

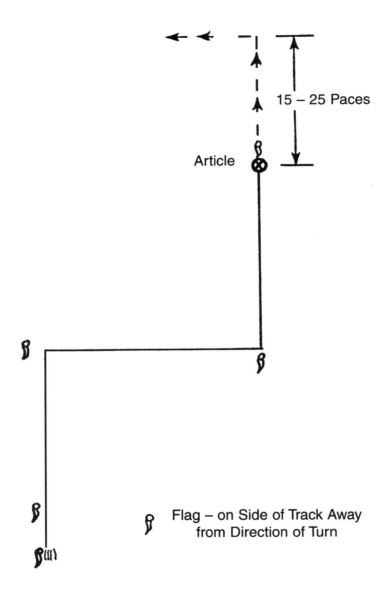

15 – 25 Paces

Article

Flag – on Side of Track Away
from Direction of Turn

Figure 10 • **Positioning Training Flags**

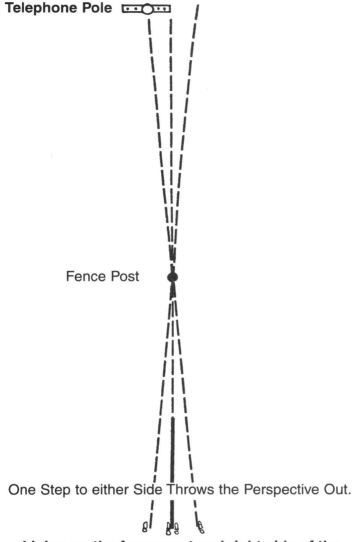

Telephone Pole

Fence Post

One Step to either Side Throws the Perspective Out.

**Lining up the fence post and right side of the
telephone pole ensures a straight line track
that will not veer to either side.**

Figure 11 • **Laying the Straight Track**

full instructions by the handler as to how the track is to be laid. A total novice once laid a track for my TDX dog because he wanted to see what a tracking dog looked like when tracking. He proceeded without any detailed instructions. Imagine the consternation when my dog executed the first three turns before he had taken out the 40 foot line I was using. The entire track, only four hundred yards in length was worked out in this manner, with about thirty turns in this short length. This would have been devastating for a novice handler and dog.

I have the reputation of being rather critical of the performance of student track layers and believe everyone teaching dogs to track should be just as critical. The track is your major tool when training dogs to track. Many times I have terminated a student handler's track for them when I see the track layer attempting to identify markers from his map with an air of doubt or hesitation and sent the track layer to retrieve his glove while I take the handler and his dog to run another track that I would lay. Once, in an attempt to avoid my rather biting criticism, a track layer deposited a couple of large tobacco leaves at each turn in an open stubble field that was almost void of natural markers. Imagine the puzzled expression of the handler when she noted that the dog was making its turns where these large tobacco leaves were appearing.

Lead Handling in Restrictive Tracking

The dog really doesn't have that much to learn in order to track, but the handler has a tremendous amount to learn before he can even adequately handle a tracking dog. During the tracking training itself, the dog has only to learn the following three things:

1. When the harness goes on and the command to track is given, there is actually something out there to be found.

2. The only way he can be successful at locating that "something" that is out there is by following that scent which always leads to the object of his search.

---

3. If he uses his nose to follow that scent, he will always locate the object of his search.

The handler, on the other hand, has to learn how to prepare his dog ahead of time; when to put on the harness; how to start the dog on a track; how to handle the dog when the dog is either on the track, loses the track, or is searching for the track; and how to interpret the dog's actions when the dog is engaged on a track. He has to learn how to keep the dog from tangling up in the tracking line; how to aid the dog in difficult terrain where the handler cannot go; and most important of all, to trust and believe the dog at all times rather than resorting to logic and guesswork that usually results in an unsuccessful track. The trained dog knows where the track goes, but the handler does not. This one single characteristic of good handling is where the vast majority of handlers fall down.

The first rule in handling the fully-trained tracking dog is to put on the harness and tracking line moments before he is to start on a track. The trained dog knows what it means when the harness is put on and will probably start looking for a track immediately, even before a command is issued. When the dog has completed a track and has been praised, the harness should come off so that he knows he is finished. Let the dog know that the harness means business, and he's to work whenever it goes on.

The second rule is to ensure the tracking line is untangled and straightened out for use before you take the dog up to the starting position of a track. Once this has been accomplished, snap the line onto his collar and take him to the starting position where you can put on the harness. Remove his collar and snap the line onto his harness. The reason for removing the collar is twofold. First, it lets him know that no enforced obedience commands are forthcoming and, secondly, you don't want the collar banging him under the chin when he has his head down, concentrating on the track.

When starting the dog, allow him the opportunity to take scent as you approach the starting flag. Should he take scent at the start, give him the command to track and let him go. Should he not take starting scent, place him in a *down* position with his head beside the starting flag and allow him several seconds before you reach down to touch the ground in front of him, commanding him to search for the track. Should he start taking scent before you can touch the ground, simply give him the command and let him start on the track.

This procedure is essential if he is to go on to TDX because there is only one flag used in TDX to indicate the start of the track. You will have no idea which direction the track layer took from the starting flag, and it will be up to the dog to determine direction of the track by himself. Walking between the first two flags seems to be a commonplace method of handling dogs at the start.

When the dog begins to move out on the track, the handler should remain stationary, allowing the dog to take out the tracking line from the right hand, which is extended out in front and the left hand, which is held down and slightly behind the handler. The line should be passing through both hands with the left hand feeling for the first knot that is located at the thirty foot mark. Once the handler feels the knot passing through his left hands, he should quickly step out in the direction the dog is taking and wrap the line around his right hand, gripping it tightly. Should the dog stop, lose the track, or come back to the handler, he should stop immediately. In this manner, the handler has not fouled the track between himself and the second flag, and, should it be necessary to restart the dog, he doesn't have to worry about the dog's being confused by his own track obliterating the track the dog is to follow.

When the dog has moved out past the second stake, the handler should settle into a fast walk, keeping the line taut between the dog and his right hand, which should be held high enough to allow the dog to circle on the spot without tangling himself up in the line. Should the dog stop for any reason whatever, the handler should also stop while maintaining a taut line. If the dog begins to cast in a circle, or come back toward the handler, the right hand should be held high and open, while the left hand pulls the slack line through the right hand, dropping the excess line onto the ground at the handler's feet. In this

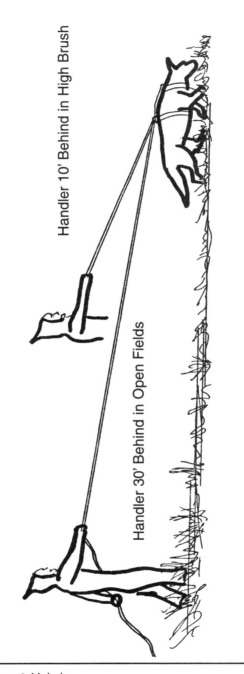

Handler 10' Behind in High Brush

Handler 30' Behind in Open Fields

Figure 12 • Lead Handling When on Track

manner, the handler can remain stationary even when the dog runs in circles around him without tangling in the line, as long as the line is taut and runs directly from the upheld right hand to the harness. When the dog indicates that he has discovered the new direction of the track, or resumes the track ahead, the handler should play out the line without moving until the knot passes once more through the left hand.

When following behind the dog at the thirty foot mark, the handler should be watching the dog's behavior for any deviation from the normal, while using the left hand to keep the line from snagging. Should it appear as if the track is going through heavy underbrush ahead, the handler should move up on the line until he is about ten feet or less behind the dog. If the dog commits himself to a track that is going through the underbrush, the handler has time to see if he an make it through with the dog. If he can't make it through where the dog is going, he can drop the tracking line, pick out a spot where he can get through, let the dog pull the light line through after him and, once through, the handler should be able to pick up the end of the tracking line without having interfered with the dog's progress. When the handler picks up the line, he should ensure that the dog will not feel a jerk should it tangle, pulling it free from a tangle himself while the dog is working. Once taught restrictive tracking, the size of the dog has no bearing whatever as far as his ability to lean into the harness and pull is concerned. It is rather obvious to spectators, and judges alike, when a dog taught restrictive tracking has come from our classes because all the dogs lean into the harness and pull and most handlers handle in the same manner. Irish Wolfhounds, German Shepherds, Shetland Sheepdogs and Toy Poodles lean into their harnesses and pull the line taut. One handler and dog team went to the extreme at a test when the handler restricted the Toy Poodle so much that the dog completed half the track on its hind legs. Needless to say, the dogs trained in this manner are difficult to pull off track when they know they are right.

I have seen countless dogs pulled off a track by their handlers at licensed tracking tests. The dog will perform well up to the turn, indicate loss of track right on the money and, when it

Figure 13 • **Lead Handling When Dog Circles**

indicates the correct direction of the turn, the handler DOESN'T believe him and refuses to follow. At one test, I watched a Cocker Spaniel pulled off the correct direction four times in a row before the dog finally went in the direction that the handler wanted it to go in, resulting in the disqualification whistle. One handler from my classes refused to believe his German Shepherd dog when it indicated the new direction of a track. Twice the dog attempted to go the right way against the handler's better judgment. He circled wide around the handler, took a mad run in the correct direction and pulled the stumbling handler off his feet. This is the attitude we want to develop in the dog. The lead is not a corrective device, and when he is right, the dog should disregard the handler and pull like mad.

The trained tracking dog will invariably tell the handler everything that has happened on a track, but only the best handlers who have the ability to interpret the dog's behavior will respond to the dog's communication. When a handler practices restrictive tracking, he can visually observe any changes in the dog's behavior, as well as feeling any deviation in pressure on the taut line. What he does when those changes are felt or seen makes the difference between a handler that is simply an interested spectator going for a run behind his dog and a handler that is truly part of a tracking team. I am always fascinated when I see my tracking students respond to their dogs' identification of a deliberately dropped business card on the second leg of a TD type of track by halting, waiting, then commanding the dogs to resume tracking without ever going over to investigate what the dogs are obviously telling the handlers is an article of some sort. This technique is effective when attempting to get students of tracking to be more aware of their dogs' behavior on a track.

Lead handling is definitely a skill that requires constant practice on the part of the handler. I've discovered that the skills of the fully-trained dog deteriorate very slowly. Though laid off tracking for almost a year, a good TDX dog doesn't forget how to track, but their handlers certainly do forget how to handle. My own deficiencies in handling after a period of not working at tracking are astounding, and it does take a period of time and effort before it comes back, as does any unpracticed skill.

Now that we have a little better understanding of some of the essentials of tracking training, the equipment requirements, and a basic idea of how the fully trained dog should be handled, let's take a look at the actual tracking training program and see how we go about training dogs in TD and TDX.

Problems

Tracking Dog Theory & Methods

TD
Training
Methods

4

Dogs starting into this training program are in training for TDX from the first day. The concepts of starting, handling and training are designed in such a manner that a dog and handler may naturally continue through both TD and TDX. This program is a structured program with definite objectives for every training session. Of all the possible errors that can be committed by students following this program, the most dangerous is jumping ahead on the schedule. Regardless of how well a dog performs during any stage of training in this program, the handler must realize before he starts that the aim of the game is behavior modification. This requires that the dog master many different situations under conditions that have many variables. There is no substitute for experience and the dog must progress in logical, small steps, or he may find himself in a situation that he has never experienced because of leaping ahead. This simple rule applies to the handler, as well, for he must acquire certain skills while advancing the training of the dog.

Before embarking on the program, it should be realized that, in order to be successful, certain rules of conduct on the part of the handler should be observed at all times when in the field training.

1. This program is totally inducive. There must be NO scolding or reprimands used when tracking. Physical abuse will almost guarantee failure.

2. Weather is no criteria for tracking. Once the schedule is started, it should be followed, regardless of the weather.

3. No forms of obedience commands should ever be used when training the dog to track, with the single exception of the *down* command, which is employed at the start of a track. If the dog doesn't already know this command, it should be taught away from the area you are tracking in.

I can recall one handler and dog that had the good fortune to go through the entire TD portion of the training program without ever having to track in adverse weather conditions. Then it happened. One of the first TDX sessions after the track had been laid, it began to rain. The handler called her Shetland Sheepdog out of the car and proceeded to head to the starting flag when the little dog stopped, looked up at the rain coming down for a few moments, and then proceeded to walk back to the car. The little dog was very reluctant to work in the rain through lack of experience, yet it did manage to obtain its TDX. Never use rain as an excuse. The dog needs this type of experience in order to handle the day when he may have to track in the rain.

Many people seem to think that rain will obliterate a track, making it virtually impossible for a dog to detect. No so. As a matter of fact, a light rain or heavy dew will freshen the track and make it easier for the dog to detect. Once, it began to rain as the track layers started their more than 1,000 yard long tracks. It poured down for three solid hours, so heavy that a person would become soaked to the skin within seconds of going outside, and small lakes appeared in the fields where we were to track. The judge apologized to us for having to fail us before we started, for "no dog would be able to track after that rain". In fact, he didn't even bring his maps along with him, as he believed the dogs wouldn't even start, and that he would be returning indoors in a few minutes.

The first dog put his nose to the ground, taking off at a fast trot in the direction of the track, as if his nose were tied to a rail, with the judge running behind muttering aloud, "It's impossible. It's impossible. No dog can track in this." The track was completed in record time. The second dog, my own, performed in the same manner as did the third dog which, unfortunately failed at the last turn, due to bad handling on the part of the owner. These dogs had performed after an incredible three hours of heavy rain, so a storm shouldn't affect the track of a dog that is in the beginning stages of the tracking program. If you expect your dog to be able to work scent in adverse conditions, you'll have to ensure that he receives training in those same adverse conditions.

Probably the best example of dogs working in scent work during highly adverse conditions was when we were working the ninety-four mile long natural gas pipeline during the month of March. We started just before daybreak when the temperature was about four degrees above zero. A storm had just begun and the wind velocity kept increasing until we were getting gusts of about thirty miles per hour. Most of the time I had to walk with my back to the oncoming wind, while the dog had to work straight into the wind. When he would have occasion to look at me, I could not see his face for the heavy layer of snow that had accumulated on his muzzle, head and eyes, which I had to keep removing. Even under these unbelievable conditions he found sixteen leaks that day, one of which he detected, broke from my directional command to run up ahead of me about two hundred yards, and commence his digging. Had he never received any training under bad weather conditions, I am certain that he would not have worked under these conditions.

Before starting this program, you will need a track layer who, ideally, is another tracking trainee and preferably a stranger to the dog. I do not believe in the handler laying his own track when training the dog to track. Once the tracks are aging more than an hour, this is permissible, but it poses certain problems for a great number of dogs. The dogs smell their owners every day, whereas a stranger's scent seems to possess a greater motivational force in getting the dogs to search for their track. Quite often you will see dogs that are trained on their owner's tracks refuse to make the transition from their handler's tracks to a stranger's track. It seems to me that it saves a lot of problems by starting the dogs on a stranger's track so that this transition is unnecessary. Should you find it impossible to get another tracking enthusiast to assist with the track laying, you could offer to pay a student to lay the tracks, according to your instructions, or, if necessary, use a husband, wife, brother, sister or child. Failing that, you'll have to lay the tracks yourself. If you can't eat steak when you are hungry, then you may have to settle for beans.

The Game

One exercise that is fun for both the dog and handler should be played whenever the opportunity presents itself. This is the "hide and seek" game, where the handler leaves the dog either on a *stay* command or has someone hold him while the handler disappears out of sight about one hundred yards away. Once out of sight behind trees or underbrush, the handler should turn at right angles to his original path and proceed an additional one hundred yards, at which point the handler is to lie down on the ground and call the dog once. The person holding the dog releases him, and the handler does not make another sound while the dog is searching for him, unless the dog turns and heads the wrong way. A second call then is in order, followed by immediate silence. The handler must not make a sound, while the dog is searching, but should be prepared to call again if it looks like he is going to take off in the wrong direction. This will force the dog to use his nose to find the handler. He will, in all probability, search for the handler with his head high, trying to detect body odor rather than resorting to tracking.

It is rather comical when I think back about dogs performing this exercise that passed within a few feet of their owners without ever discovering them when the wind was blowing from the handler away from the dog. Instead of using their noses to find their handlers, they relied upon their eyesight, which in dogs happens to be quite ineffective when the object of their search remains stationary. Even more humorous was the Toy Poodle that did locate its owner by scent, but became overly suspicious and downright hostile when he made visual contact of the owner who was in a prostrate position on the ground. The dog's antics became more frenetic when the handler called to him. You could see the tremendous emotional conflict the dog was experiencing when hearing the familiar voice, smelling the familiar smell, but seeing the handler in this prostrate position , which he had never seen before. His sense of smell and hearing pulled him toward his handler until his sight told him that this sublime figure wasn't the source of his search. Once the handler stood up, all doubt was erased and the little Toy Poodle happily closed the distance.

The game is fun for both handler and dog, but in most cases, it seems to aid the majority of dogs in tracking training very little. Occasionally, it seems to help with certain types of problem dogs when extra motivation to use their noses is required, but this is the exception rather than the rule. You won't know whether or not this game will have any benefit, simply because you won't know if your dog is the type of problem dog we've described. Since the game has no detrimental value, I would strongly suggest that it be employed regularly during the first few weeks of training right after completing a training session.

The First Week of Training

Having selected the area you are going to do your training in, plus all of the necessary equipment mentioned in the previous chapter, begin the training as follows:

1. Put the harness on your dog, clip on the tracking line and select one of the articles you are going to use. Try to get your dog excited over the article, and as you throw it, send your dog after it. Couple this with whatever command you're going to use for tracking. Praise him profusely when he picks it up, not

---

The handler excites the dog with the article.

The handler throws the article into the wind.

The command to track is given
and the handler follows the dog.

Track layer excites the dog with the article.

Track layer throws article into the wind.

The handler commands the dog to track, and follows.

when he returns it. The purpose here is to identify and not necessarily retrieve it. Should he happen to return with it, continue the vigorous praise. Throw the article out several times and follow behind him about six to ten feet on the line. Do not attempt to restrict him in any way. When he picks up the article, praise him and drop to one knee and coax him into bringing it back to you. The article that will probably work the best is a glove that is rolled to form a sort of leather tube with a couple of elastic bands to hold its shape. Should the dog show a lack of interest in going after the glove, he is not a natural retriever, and the retrieve will not provide the motivation necessary to train him as a tracking dog. Don't panic. The non-retriever can be taught to track with this same training program. You'll simply have to use some other motivational force to get him interested in looking for a track. If you are a handler that has a non-retriever, look at the end of this chapter, following the WEEK 10 TRAINING SCHEDULE for the motivational section and by using the same schedule and training methods, coupled with the NON-RETRIEVER chart, continue the training. For the purpose of simplification, I will continue as though your dog is a natural retriever, but please understand that this same program is used to produce TD and TDX dogs that do not retrieve.

More than 50% of dogs entering our tracking training program are non-retrievers, yet are usually the first dogs to earn their tracking titles. The compulsive retrieving instinct, or the absence of it seems to have little bearing on the dog's ability to become a good tracking dog.

2. After the dog has retrieved the article several times in the manner detailed, repeat the same process with the track layer, getting the dog excited in the glove, throwing it and following the dog as he retrieves it. Repeat this process several times before continuing on to the next step, and should the dog's interest wane, categorize him as a non-retriever for the purpose of training and refer to the section in this chapter which covers the non-retriever.

3. After completing the many retrieves as explained in 1

and 2, have the track layer place a stake in the ground while you hold the dog about one pace downwind of the track layer. The track layer should attempt to get the dog excited in the glove once more and should walk into the wind about five paces, while throwing the glove into the air and playing with it. At the end of the five paces, he should turn to face the dog, throw the glove into the air while calling the dog by name and then place it on the ground at his feet. As soon as the handler sees the glove hit the ground, he is to give the dog the command to track and follow behind the dog at the dog's pace. When the dog retrieves (indicates) the glove, the handler should immediately drop to one knee and praise him.

4. The track layer should now place a stake into the ground a few paces upwind of where the dog found the glove in the previous exercise. The dog is to be held back about one pace downwind of the stake, slightly to its right. The track layer now performs as he did in the previous exercise, walking into the wind while throwing the glove into the air and playing with it all the time. Counting off his paces, the track layer should continue in this manner for ten paces, place a stake into the ground immediately in front of him, turn to face the dog, call the dog by name, throw the glove into the air and make it obvious to the dog that he is placing the glove on the ground in front of him directly on his track and then retrace his steps back to the stake. When he arrives at the starting stake, he should step to the left of the stake and without a word, continue a few paces past the handler. At the moment the track layer passes the handler, the handler should issue the command to track and follow the dog, at the dog's pace, six to ten feet behind the dog.

5. Having completed Step 4, the track layer should place the starting flag into the ground a few feet beyond the last stake, which is the one he used to mark the article drop. Performing in the same manner as described in Step 4, the track layer should count his steps into the wind and, at the ten pace mark, stop to place a second stake into the ground about an arm's length to the left of the track. He then continues out to the twenty pace mark, where he places the article drop stake into the ground in

front of him. After placing the stake, he turns to face the dog, calls his name, throws the article into the air and, with a great display, places it on the track in front of him. Once again the track layer returns past the handler, who starts his dog at the moment the track layer steps past him. In this manner, the handler and track layer have completed the first day of tracking in accordance with the schedule on the next page, but this does not complete the first day's work. The first week of tracking training is shown in table form (as is the remainder of the program) but the first week's schedule, which calls for three tracks per day is to be repeated three times each day for a total of nine tracks per day. Therefore, it is time to follow the first day's schedule and repeat the track twice more.

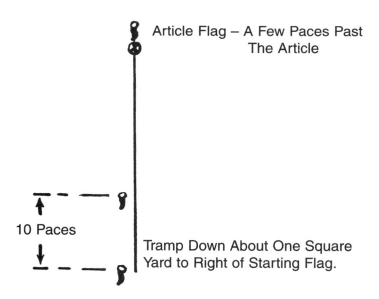

Article Flag – A Few Paces Past The Article

10 Paces

Tramp Down About One Square Yard to Right of Starting Flag.

Figure 14 • **First Week Track Design**

First Week Tracking Training Chart

Day	Track	Distance (YDS.)	Wind Direction	Lay
1	1	5	Into	D
	2	10	Into	D
	3	20	Into	D
2	1	10	Into	D
	2	20	Into	D
	3	40	Into	D
3	1	20	Into	D
	2	40	With	D
	3	80	With	D
4	1	40	With	D
	2	80	With	D
	3	160	With	D
5	1	80	With	D
	2	160	With	S
	3	320	With	S
6	1	160	With	S
	2	320	With	S
	3	400	With	S

D = Double laid track. The Track layer goes out and returns by the same route. The dog is started when the Track layer has returned.

S = Single laid track. The Track layer goes out, but does not return along the same route. The dog isn't started until the Track layer returns to the handler.

Track layer excites the dog with the article
before walking Into the wind.

Track layer obtains the dogs attention
before dropping the article

Track layer excites the dog with the article
before walking Into the wind.

You'll find out early in the training of a dog that he is prone to use his eyes and memory to mentally mark an article dropped by the track layer. This will also be noticed when you throw a ball out into a field and send the dog to find it. The dog will run out to the point where he has mentally marked its position to be with his head high. Once that point is reached, he will drop his head and resort to using his nose to locate it. This distance will vary from dog to dog, but it is usually about the fifty to eighty yard mark. In the beginning, when he can see the article being dropped, he will not be tracking until he has reached this mark. Once his nose is down, he will quickly discover that the scent of the track layer always leads to the object of his search.

The handler must remember that the purpose of this first week of training is simply to get across to the dog that when we say there is something out there, there really is something out there, and that we are going to go along with him when he tries to locate it. As the tracks become longer, the handler should run behind his dog at the pace set by the dog, playing out more and more of the tracking line as the dog goes. Under no condition is the handler to leave the actual track. Should the dog start to veer off the track by more than a few feet, the handler should slow down until the dog comes back onto the track. The handler should not come to a sudden halt when the dog starts to veer off the actual track, but should start increasing the tension on the line and finally come to a halt if he continues to go off the track. In this manner, the forward progress of both the handler and dog occurs only when the dog is actually on the track.

The track layer, by returning along the same path he went out on, is laying a double-laid track. As the length of the track increases, so does its age, as well as the length of time between the dog seeing the drop and going after it. This means that the longer the track, the more the dog has to rely on memory. By the time the dog is working on a four hundred yard track, he has had a good ten minutes between the actual drop and the command to locate it. The handler should watch carefully when the track is being laid, so that he will know exactly where the track is located, especially if the track layer lays the track in a curve,

which many are prone to do. By the end of the week, the tracks
will be so long that the handler will probably be unable to see
the article flag until he has proceeded behind the dog for a good
portion of the track, necessitating careful watching where the
track layer actually went.

The Tracking Training Schedule – Week 1

The tracking training schedule calls for three different
tracks that must be laid in sequence – and tracked in the same
sequence. Once completed, the same three tracks are repeated a
second time and then a third time. It is of critical importance to
follow the schedule exactly as detailed, especially the distances
stipulated and the wind direction, with respect to the track at the
time the dog is to track. Should the track layer lay the track correctly, but a wind direction change occurs before the dog goes
on the track, it must be discarded and a new track laid. Do not
expect the dog to track with his head down at this stage. The
scent of the track, or possibly the scent from the article itself
will be blowing directly into the dog's head making it possible
for the dog to move accurately in the correct direction with
head held high.

By laying the track into the wind, we are making it
extremely easy for the dog to smell the track or the article and
are preventing him from trailing or fringe following from the
start. Observe the dog's actions closely, especially when there is
a slight shift in the wind's direction to see if he has the tendency to drift several paces off the track on its downwind side. This
may forewarn you of tendencies to trail. On the longer tracks,
watch for repeated tendencies of the dog to demonstrate waning
interest, especially on the third section of tracks or even the second. Should his interest decrease on the third section of repeated tracks, cut the sections down to two. Should it appear on the
second section, cut him down to one. Some dogs cannot take
this heavy training load. The dogs that make the best trackers
will be able to handle it.

When the schedule calls for single laid tracks, ensure that
the track layer continues on past the last article flag for at least
fifteen to twenty-five paces before he leaves the track to return

Correct distance from starting flag to put harness on.

Place dog in a down position by starting flag.

Touch the start to get the dog to take scent.

When the dog starts, the handler simply plays out line.

The dog reaches the 10 yard training flag
before the handler moves out beyond him.

to the handler. His return path should not bring him any closer than fifty paces to the actual track on its downwind side. Once he has returned to the handler, the dog should be started and the track layer should continue to follow behind the handler at a distance of about fifty paces. Having given the dog the command to track, the handler should not say anything to the dog when it is actually working or looking for the track. Encouragement or praise at this time can result in distracting the dog, causing him to break off what he is doing to return to the handler for more praise or encouragement. Many dogs have problem handlers that constantly talk the poor dog to death, rather than allowing him to do his job.

One student handler in my classes had this terrible tendency to talk too much to the dog, coupled with a lack of faith in what the dog was doing. In order to correct this habit, I launched a tirade at her when she started to jabber away at her dog when he was looking for a turn in the track. I hollered at the handler, "If you don't stop talking and start believing, I'll tape your mouth shut, blindfold you, tie your hands behind your back and snap the line onto your belt and then the dog will do a proper job of tracking." Needless to say, it worked, and as long as I was behind her, the problem disappeared. Let it suffice to say that I firmly believe that a highly critical track layer following behind the handler is an asset to the dog's progress, as well as the handler's.

The Tracking Schedule — Week 2

During the first week of tracking, the dog has been started on the track from any position that he is in when the track layer has returned. Starting the second week, the handler is to insist the dog be kept in a place where he can see the track layer going out, but not immediately behind the starting position. Once the track layer returns, the handler is to bring the dog up to the starting point and give him the command to start. Should the dog start sniffing at any point when approaching the starting flag, allow him to do so, giving him the command to start when he arrives at the start. Taking adequate starting scent is of critical importance and should the dog not be allowed to take sufficient scent from the start, you can expect problems to develop. If the dog hasn't visibly taken any scent, the handler should reach down and run his fingers through the grass below the dog's nose while saying in a quizzical manner, "What's this?" in an attempt to interest the dog in the area of the track before standing up and commanding him to "Find it!"

Second Week Tracking Training Chart

Day	Track	Distance (Yds..)	Wind Direction	Lay	Age
1	1	5	With	S	5 Min.
	2	10	With	S	5 Min.
	3	20	With	S	5 Min.
2	1	10	With	S	8 Min.
	2	20	With	S	8 Min.
	3	40	With	S	8 Min.
3	1	20	With	S	10 Min.
	2	40	With	S	10 Min.
	3	80	With	S	10 Min.
4	1	40	With	S	15 Min
	2	80	With	S	15 Min
	3	160	With	S	15 Min
5	1	80	With	S	15 Min.
	2	160	With	S	15 Min.
	3	320	With	S	15 Min.
6	1	160	With	S	15 Min.
	2	320	With	S	15 Min.
	3	400	With	S	15 Min.

S = Single laid track. The Track layer goes out, but does not return by the same route. The return route should be downwind at least 50 yards.

Some dogs, especially those that are young or have had no previous training, will want to run during the first two weeks. Should this be the case, let him run. If the dog normally does things slowly, or if he has been trained a great deal in obedience compulsively, he will probably not run, and you will not alter this type of behavior in tracking. A slow dog will remain slow, while a fast dog will work fast.

By now, the question will be raised about whether you will have to track every day and what happens if you miss a day? The ideal situation is where the dog is trained every day for six days and rested one. Should you miss a day for some reason, simply resume where you left off. I have never attempted to run a dog and handler through this program any other way, and can only surmise what would happen if you trained only a couple of days per week. You would probably be all right as song as no scheduled days training were missed, but that is only supposition. If you want to train a tracking dog, you'd best make up your mind to commit the time and effort so that he is prepared properly in the time span allocated.

During this second week, the dog will be tracking with the wind blowing away from him, which will start to bring his head down since the track's scent is now blowing away from him. He'll not be able to detect it as easily with his head held high. Observe his behavior carefully, especially when there is a sudden change in wind direction to a crosswind to see if he tries to trail, rather than track. The age of the track is determined by timing the absence of the track layer from the moment he steps off the starting flag. The track layer must ensure at this stage that he tramples down about a square yard of vegetation at the right of the starting flag. This is where the dog will be given the maximum opportunity to take starting scent. From that point, the track layer should step out normally without dragging his feet.

When the dog begins to move out on the track the handler should watch his progress and start moving after the dog as he passes the second flag all the while playing out the tracking line until the knot makes its presence known in the handler's left hand.

During this second week of training, the sequence of nine tracks is to be followed, except that the first three tracks should be laid first and then the dog tracked on them in the same sequence.

The Tracking Schedule – Week 3

By this time, the dog will believe the handler when he is told that there is something out there to be found when the command to "Find it" is given. He will realize that the strange smell he has been encountering does, in fact, lead to the object of his search. Now he is ready to attempt the first turn. Dogs that aren't specifically taught how to navigate a turn may eventually catch on, but if taught properly, will be performing the turn within the first week of training for turns. The key to training dogs to execute the turn is in the second leg's direction with respect to the wind and its strength compared to the first leg.

The second leg must be laid into the wind so that the scent of the track (and the article in the beginning) will be blown towards him. By triple laying this second leg, it will be overpowering in scent strength and easily detectable by the dog. Since the dog has the natural tendency to circle to his right, the second leg must also be a right turn so that the length of time that the dog has actually lost the track when passing the turn is minimal. In this manner, he will not have time to become discouraged before rediscovering the track. The article is only a short distance from the turn and will reinforce the dog's actions almost immediately after discovering the new direction.

When the track layer is laying this first turn, he should come to a halt after the designated number of paces, reach out an arm's length and place the corner stake in the ground. Now he should turn to his right, proceed the designated distance in the new direction, come to a halt, place the glove underfoot, reach out in front of himself and place the article stake in the ground. By turning around, he will see the corner stake and move toward it until he is one pace away, make another about turn and continue to walk over the glove, sidestepping the article stake and continuing on for at least fifteen paces before turning to leave the track area.

The dog should be left in the car while the track is being laid or in a place where the dog cannot see the track being laid. From this point on in his tracking training, he will never see the track being laid unless he runs into a problem that is discussed under PROBLEMS at the end of this book.

When approaching the starting flag, the harness should be put on the dog about ten to fifteen paces before the starting flag. From this point, the handler should snap the lead onto the harness and, while approaching the starting flag, allow the dog

Third Week Tracking Training Chart

Day	Track	First Leg (Yds.)	Second Leg (Yds.)	Wind	Lay	Age
1	1	100	20	Into	T	15 Min.
	2	100	40	Into	T	15 Min.
	3	100	80	Into	T	15 Min.
2	1	125	40	Into	Ss	15 Min.
	2	125	80	Into	Ss	15 Min.
	3	125	160	Into	Ss	15 Min.
3	1	140	80	Into	S	15 Min.
	2	160	160	Into	S	15 Min.
	3	200	200	Into	S	15 Min.
4	1	100	20	With	T	15 Min.
	2	100	40	With	T	15 Min.
	3	100	80	With	T	15 Min.
5	1	125	40	With	Ss	15 Min.
	2	125	80	With	Ss	15 Min.
	3	125	160	With	Ss	15 Min.
6	1	140	80	With	S	15 Min.
	2	160	160	With	S	15 Min.
	3	200	200	With	S	15 Min.

Wind — Refers to the direction of the second leg with respect to the wind

T = Triple lay (Second leg only)

Ss = Toe to heel stepping on second leg only

S = Single lay throughout both legs

a couple yards of lead in case he might detect the track. The moment the dog arrives at the start, he should be given the command, only if he has detected and is following the track. If he doesn't place the dog in a *down* position with his head beside the flag, wait several seconds and then reach down, run your finger through the grass and start him the moment he takes scent. Should he take scent at any time after being placed down with a command, he should receive the command to track. When the dog starts, the handler should remain at the start until the dog has moved out in a straight line, obviously on the track until the thirty foot knot is felt in the left hand. At that moment, the handler should move out at the dog's pace, wrap the line around the right hand and slowly increase the tension until a fast walking pace is reached.

During the first three days of training in week three, the pattern No. 1 on the next page is to be used when laying out the tracks. For the latter three days, pattern No. 2 is to be used. The specified wind direction always refers to the second leg of the track and all tracks are to be fifteen minutes old. Instead of the nine tracks per day as specified in weeks 1 and 2, only the specified three tracks per day are to be worked out by the dog.

You will probably notice that the dog will run past the turn a short distance before realizing that the track scent is no longer present. Should he want to keep going past the corner stake, the handler is not to stop him. Continue to follow the dog in the direction he is going until either the dog stops or the handler arrives at the corner stake, at which time the handler is to go no further. Do not turn to face the direction that the track is going to take. Stand still, facing in the direction you were going, until the dog has found the new direction and is committed to follow it. Should the dog either not look for the new direction or give up entirely, simply take a few steps in the new direction with him. Encourage him to find it all the way until he picks it up and moves out on his own.

Most dogs will notice the loss quickly and when they circle back to find it, or to act puzzled, they act very surprised to find the new direction is stronger than that which they were originally following. They have the tendency to accelerate down the second leg with a great burst of speed. As long as the dog hasn't quit looking for the track, the handler should remain immobile without assisting the dog in any manner whatever. At this point some may think that the dog is going to learn to spot the stakes which mark the corners and article drop, which he may do. It really doesn't matter because the stakes will be coming down very soon.

During this week of training the dog will be tracking the first leg of the track with a crosswind and the handler must watch for the tendency to track several yards downwind of the track at this time. As the dog starts to drift downwind of the

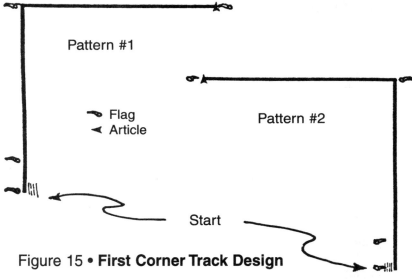

Figure 15 • **First Corner Track Design**

Corner Flags – Always places on the opposite side of the track, to where the Track layer is about to head.

T = Triple lay. The Track layer goes, returns and then goes out on the track again, meaning that he has passed over the same ground three different times

Ss = Single, short step lay. The Track layer moves out a single lay, but moves his feet in a heel-to-toe fashion.

S = Single lay.

Tracking Dog Theory & Methods

When at a turn, the handler stands still, keeping the line running
from his upraised hand to the harness so that the
dog cannot wrap the line around his legs or the handler's legs,
allowing the slack line to drop onto the ground.

track, simply increase the tension on the line and, if necessary, come to a halt until he gets back on the track. There is absolutely nothing to gain by eating up the track yourself that the dog should be following and allowing him to parallel the track several yards downwind of the track which will make him a trailer, or worse still, a fringe follower. The handler must practice lead handling at this point, maintaining a taut line when the dog is tracking, halting as soon as the dog's behavior changes upon arrival at the corner flag. When following behind the dog, the handler should allow for the crosswind by permitting the dog to continue on the track even if there is a tendency to track up to six feet off the actual track. The more off the track the dog is, the greater the tension on the line should be. Should the dog attempt to move off the track by more than six feet, the handler should come to a halt.

Keep the line running down from the right hand to the harness without it ever touching the ground between the handler and the dog. Release the excess line he has taken in onto the ground when the dog heads toward the handler. Should the dog become tangled in the line, realize that it was because of poor lead handling. Call the dog to you and then untangle him. Do not go up to the dog because you may either foul the track or be unable to return to the spot you left when the stakes are down.

The Tracking Schedule – Week 4
Starting the fourth week of training heralds the second turn and the dog will have to execute both right and left turns, all of which cannot be laid into the wind. In other words, he'll have to handle the second leg of the track with a crosswind. During the previous week the dog may have had the tendency to cut a corner without tracking right up to the actual turn. Should he want to cut the corner by a few paces, let him do it. He may have caught wind of either the second leg of the track or the article itself blowing to him. He may also have been tracking a little downwind during the latter three days of the schedule and come across the new leg of the track without having actually touched the corner. Should this happen, and it will happen more often now that the number of turns are increasing, do not run up

Fourth Week Tracking Training Chart

Day	Track	Weak Leg	Length(Yds.)	Wind	Lay	Age
1	1	1	100	Into	S	15 Min.
		2	75	cross	Sb	15 Min.
		3	25	Into	T	15 Min.
	2	1	100	Into	S	15 Min.
		2	100	cross	Sb	15 Min.
		3	50	Into	T	15 Min.
	3	1	125	Into	S	15 Min.
		2	125	cross	Sb	15 Min.
		3	100	Into	Ss	15 Min.
2	1	1	100	Into	S	15 Min.
		2	75	cross	Sb	15 Min.
		3	25	Into	Ss	15 Min.
	2	1	100	Into	S	15 Min.
		2	100	cross	Sb	15 Min.
		3	50	Into	Sb	15 Min.
	3	1	125	Into	S	15 Min.
		2	125	cross	Sb	15 Min.
		3	100	Into	Sb	15 Min.
3	1	1	100	Into	S	15 Min.
		2	75	cross	Sb	15 Min.
		3	25	Into	Sb	15 Min.
	2	1	100	Into	S	15 Min.
		2	100	cross	S	15 Min.
		3	50	Into	Sb	15 Min.
	3	1	125	Into	S	15 Min.
		2	125	cross	S	15 Min.
		3	100	Into	S	15 Min.

S = Single Lay

T = Triple Lay

Ss = Single Lay, but toe-to-heel fashion.

Sb = Single Lay, but the first 10 paces are
only heel-to-toe fashion.

*Note – The next three days repeat chart but change wind
direction of the first and third legs.*

to the turns yourself. As a handler, you are to follow behind your dog. If he cuts a corner when you know he is on the track, then you are to cut the corner right behind him.

During this week of training, observe the dog's behavior for any problems that might be developing and should they appear, do not advance to week five schedule before consulting the chapter on PROBLEMS and taking the appropriate corrective action. All of the stakes used to mark the turns are now removed from the track with the exception of the starting flag, which is still placed in the ground to the left of the track's start. The second flag's distance is now increased to thirty yards from the start. The track layer must make a map of his tracks from this point on in order to ensure that the dog is on track and to help the handler – dog team when they are in trouble. The map he prepares should contain enough information so that he can locate his track at a point along the track. He is making the map for himself, not for someone else to read, therefore, the only information contained in the map should be that which is pertinent to the track layer.

The second turn in the track is handled in the same manner as the first turn. Pattern No. 1 is the design used for the first three days of tracking on all three tracks per day with the first and third legs running into the wind. Pattern No 2 is the design used for the second three days of tracking, which has the first and third legs running with the wind. The handler must watch carefully for any tendency on the part of the dog to trail or to tire excessively during the running of the three tracks. Should the dog tire, or show a loss of interest in the third track of the day repeatedly, then the first track design and lengths should be dropped from the dog's program. This will be the last week of multiple tracks per day, and we certainly do not want to tire the dog excessively at this point.

The Tracking Schedule – Week 5

By the time you have concluded the fourth week training schedule, you could probably pass at a tracking test if you had ideal conditions, if the dog is really keen on "doing his-thing," and if you have a great deal of luck. Many of my students have

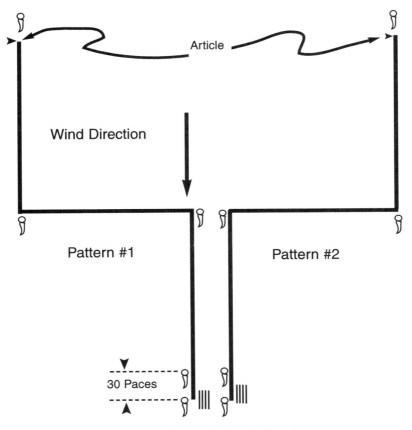

Article

Wind Direction

Pattern #1

Pattern #2

30 Paces

The Fourth Week Track Design

Figure 16 • **Second Corner Track Design**

done just this. They have entered a licensed trial that came up during their fifth week of tracking training and obtained their tracking title. I have to remind them at that point that although their dogs basically know how to track, they are far from being "Tracking Dogs." From this point on, we are primarily concerned with training the handler and helping the dog learn how to surmount the many problems he'll face when conditions are not favorable, when he is really not up to scratch and when there is no luck available.

At this stage of the dog's training, he is becoming aware of the fact that when the track scent disappears, there is probably a change in direction of the track. The handler is now looking for indications by the dog that he has lost the track when passing a corner as well as some indication by the dog of having located the track's new direction. Up to now, these indications are probably occurring when the dog is in front of the handler and the dog is becoming conditioned to look for the track's new direction somewhere between his handler and himself. Now we have to prepare the dog for the eventuality that the new direction of the track is located behind his handler. This means we will have to teach the dog to execute a full 360 degree search around the handler should he be unable to locate the track in front of the handler. This is one of the purposes of the fifth week of training.

Instituting a third turn at this stage of the dog's training will present no problem as long as he is handling the first two turns with no problems. The type of turn we are going to use in order to teach both the dog and the handler that the track's new direction may be behind the handler is the "acute angle turn." There are many who would discourage the use of an acute angle and I would have to agree with them if this angle is improperly laid. However, a properly laid acute angle when in training is the best method I have ever seen employed to teach both handler and dog how to react if there is no track out in front of the handler to be found. Great care must be executed in laying this type of track or the result will be a totally lost dog and handler.

There are three critical features of the track incorporating an acute angle that will contribute to its successful use.

1. Wind direction

2. Degree of acuteness

3. Direction of the track with respect to the wind when tracking

Ideal use of the acute angle should be at about the second or third turn of a regular track when the wind is blowing with considerable strength from behind the track layer when it is to be executed. The track layer should come to a halt, turn 90 degrees to his left and then turn 45 degrees more for a total of 135 degrees before continuing in a straight line once more. The left hand direction simply means that should the dog's tendency be to circle to his right, he will not immediately pick up the new direction of the track. In order to pick up the track, he'll have to circle almost completely around his handler. The track layer must follow closely behind the tracking team as they approach the acute angle. This will ensure that the dog doesn't overshoot the turn by such a great distance that he cannot rediscover the track by circling at the end of the lead behind the handler. The handler, on the other hand, should encourage the overshooting of the turn by allowing the dog to run the track as he approaches the acute angle.

Behavior When Tracking at an Acute Angle

When the dog is tracking a relatively fresh track (not older than fifteen minutes) with the wind at his back, he'll have the tendency to overshoot the acute turn. If the wind velocity is strong enough, the handler's ideal position, when coming to a halt, will be a short distance past the turn. Obviously the dog will not find any track in front of his handler. (see Figure 19) Should the dog not take the initiative to search behind the handler, the handler must take action. The handler should turn 90 degrees to his right and encourage the dog to search. If the dog starts to search in front of the handler again, the handler should turn another 90 degrees to his right so that he is facing the direction he has come from. If the dog searches in front of the handler once more, he will locate the track and its new direction. Figure 18 illustrates the correct lay of an acute angle while Figure 17 illustrates what can occur when it is improperly laid.

The dog that started on the improperly laid track continuing the acute angle arrived at the turn preceding the acute turn with the wind at his back and overshot the turn. This overshoot placed the dog at the next leg of the track and, being a novice dog, he backtracked the track layer until he reached the point of no return, hopelessly lost.

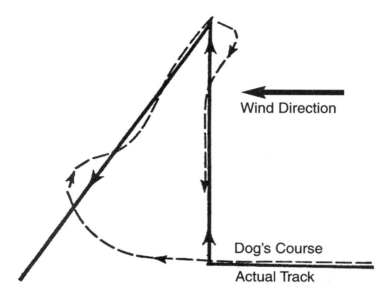

Figure 17 • **Improperly Designed Acute Angle**

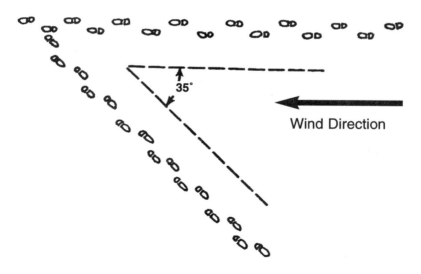

Figure 18 • **Laying the Acute Angle**

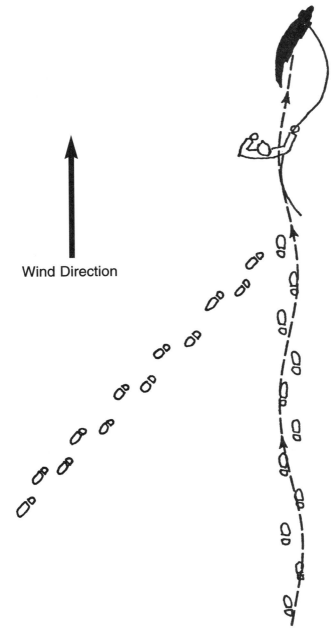

Wind Direction

Figure 19 • **Handling the Acute Angle**

Once properly trained, a dog acquires experience in his search for the track once he has lost it. This experience will modify his searching for a new track direction along a pattern that resembles this. In the beginning he will tend to pass the turn and slow down. The head will probably lift, and he will circle to the right, put his nose to the ground to search for the track. Later, having discovered that the turn is invariably between the handler and himself, he will go past the turn a few steps, come to a halt, and investigate the ground area immediately to his right and left for the track (he knows there is a turn that usually goes left or right). If he cannot find it right away, he turns 360 degrees and starts to investigate the ground area back to the handler. (He knows from experience that it always has been between the handler and himself). Should he be unsuccessful in discovering the track with this searching maneuver, he'll search the same line out from the handler to the end of the line before starting a full 360 degree scan around behind the handler to locate the track.

What a relief it has been to me to have my own dogs search in this manner when we have overshot a turn (which will occasionally happen to the best dogs and handlers) to discover the track behind me and continue on to complete the track. I have to feel sorry for those handlers whose dogs have performed well, only to get the whistle when the wind has carried them past the turn and the dog refused to swing all the way around the handler where he could have picked up the track. If the handler can keep his perspective when this occurs, and should the dog fail to swing behind the handler, then the handler should start stepping back in the direction whence he came. In this way, the dog's searching pattern will be taken back to a point where the handler knows the track to be. Here the handler is working as part of the tracking team, compensating for the dog's failure to search the entire area about the handler.

The number of tracks per day are now reduced to one, the turns are three and the time, or age of the track is increased in two steps to twenty-five minutes, which is just below the hump we are approaching. At the end of this fifth week of training, the handler and dog should attempt the "Test Track." With my

---

Tracking Dog Theory & Methods

own classes, I use the test track for two purposes, the first of which verifies whether or not the dog is, in fact, tracking. The second purpose is to build in the handler a confidence that the dog can track or cannot track and that we have a problem that must be identified and corrected.

To lay the test track, I will go to a field area without the handler and lay a regulation distance track of about 500 paces that is double laid. I will triple lay the first ten yards past each turn and include one acute angle in the design. Without telling the handler how the track was laid or any information on its pattern or what the article is, I send the tracking student out to find the article while I leave for home. The handler and dog are left totally on their own with instructions not to come back without the article. When they do return, they are to draw the design of the track, showing the number of turns, the approximate direction of each leg and return to me the article I have left at the end of the track.

I have had students out in a snowstorm for over two hours trying to find the article when the dog became lost (due to unreliable handling) and others that have returned minutes later beaming with confidence at their results. The handler and dog that performed so badly on their first test track turned out later to be the best tracking duo I have ever seen. From that day on, the handler believed her dog. There is no better way to build up a handler's confidence than by having them out in a field by themselves with no one to help them if they get lost and have them complete the track successfully. On the other hand, the students who do get lost realize now that there really is a problem, either with the dog or with their handling. Should the unsuccessful student draw a design of his progress, I can tell how far the dog went with accuracy and whether the error was a problem in the dog's tracking or an error in handling. By double and triple laying the track and by getting the student tracking team on the track when its age is only fifteen minutes, I know that should the dog be using its nose to track, he'll have no difficulty with the test track. On the other hand, trouble on the test track proves to me that we have a problem that must be determined and corrected before they can advance any further.

Throughout the fifth week of training, the wind direction with respect to any of the legs is no longer a criteria of track design, for the dog should now be exposed to varying wind conditions. His tracking area should be changed from day to day to incorporate all types of vegetation and lack of it. Should the handler discover that the dog seems to lose the track at any point and isn't able to find it again, although he is apparently searching for it, then the handler should move up to the dog, take a hold of his harness and move him in the direction of the track (as stipulated by the track layer) with encouragement to "Find it." When the dog starts to move out on his own again, the handler should play out the line and resume normal handling. He may have hit and surmounted the hump.

Fifth Week Tracking Training Chart

Day	Track	Leg 1	Leg 2	Leg 3	Leg 4	Age of Track
1	1	100	75	100	50	15 Min.
2	1	100	100	125	75	15 Min.
3	1	100	100	125	100	20 Min.
4	1	100	100	100	150	20 Min.
5	1	125	125	125	125	25 Min.
6	1	100	100	150	150	25 Min.

The Tracking Schedule – Week 6

By this time the handler can probably "taste" the T.D. title he is going after and he is confident in the knowledge that his dog is tracking. Now it is the handler's turn to learn and increase his proficiency at lead handling, as well as gaining in experience to work with his dog as a team. The tracks should be

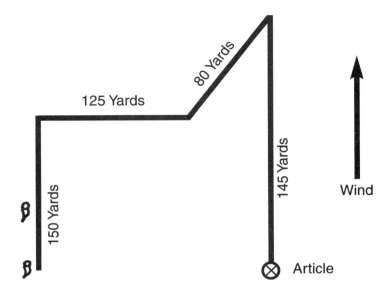

125 Yards

80 Yards

150 Yards

145 Yards

Wind

Article

Figure 20 • **The Test Track**

laid in vegetation that changes from one type to another type. The tracking areas should include stubble, pasture land, alfalfa, high weeded areas and areas where turns may be executed beside trees. Increased difficulty in terrain should be incorporated in the track design, as well as one turn that is obtuse in nature. The four turns specified should include one 90 degree turn to the left, one to the right, one acute angle and one obtuse. The handler should have no previous knowledge of the track and should start observing the dog's behavior closely when he shows a loss of track, a discovery of track, and resumption in track.

Once the dog has lost the track, either on a straight stretch (possibly due to a distraction) or on a turn, he will start to look for the track with his nose close to the ground. By observing his behavior when the dog is circling, the handler will probably notice that his course has a set speed or pace while casting for the track. When he actually passes over the track while scent-

---

ing, the handler will notice that the dog's head will suddenly be stopped, as if by an invisible fish hook that appears to have snagged the dog's nose momentarily. This behavior tells the handler that the dog has scented something different at that particular point and the handler should be watching closely for any further indication at that point of a possible track existing there. Quite often the dog will turn just past that point to come back across it again and should this same behavior occur once more, with the dog seeming to quarter across the point of discovery in ever tightening casts while starting to head out in its direction, the handler should start to follow as soon as the thirty feet of line has been taken out and the dog is heading in a straight line. This is probably the most commonly exhibited behavior of most tracking dogs when they have rediscovered a lost track.

Sixth Week Tracking Training Chart

Day	Track	Length	Corners	Corner Content	Track
1	1	4-500	4	1A-1B-2R	25 Min.
2	1	4-500	4	1A-1B-2R	25 Min.
3	1	4-500	4	1A-1B-2R	25 Min.
4	1	4-500	4	1A-1B-2R	25 Min.
5	1	4-500	4	1A-1B-2R	25 Min.
6	1	4-500	4	1A-1B-2R	25 Min.

A = Acute • B = Obtuse • R = Right Angle

The Tracking Schedule – Week 7

By the end of the sixth week of tracking, it is time to surmount the "Hump." (Described in Chapter II) As time goes on and the track age increases, there will come a time when the individual's body odor will decrease to less than that of the track scent and the dog will, in all probability, become lost

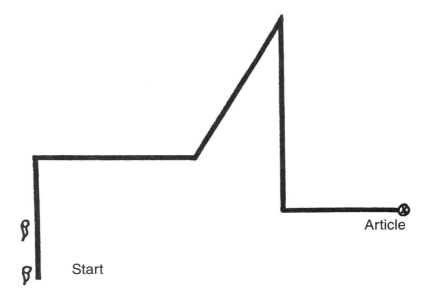

Article

Start

Figure 21 • **Typical Sixth Week Track Design**

and confused when he can no longer locate the scent he was following. Up to this point, he has been basically a trailer that we have kept close to the track. Now it is time to make a tracking dog out of him.

The design of the track during the next week should be simple, consisting of a "U" shaped track with only two turns. The distance of the tracks should be approximately three hundred yards, but each leg of the track should be different in distance. The tracks should be laid in pairs, one right after the other and with a time separation of about ten minutes between the conclusion of the first and the commencement of the second. Throughout this week increase the age of each paired tracks by five minutes, starting with the first day at twenty-five minutes. Having tracked the first track, the handler should immediately continue on to the second track. The second day, the first track laid should be thirty minutes old before the dog is put on it. At any time the dog experiences difficulty when on the track, he should be led step by step through the track's entirety unless he decides to move out on the track himself. This means that the handler must know exactly where the track is before going on it with his dog. Encouragement when leading the dog is a must and should be given without any reservation as the handler is leading the dog by the harness. Use the chart given in Chapter II to determine the approximate time point of the hump when tracking in conditions other than a hot, dry, windless day with normal vegetation and alter the age of the tracks accordingly. Once over the hump, the dog and handler are ready for the session where "reading the dog" is to be accomplished.

The Tracking Schedule – Week 8
    By the end of the seventh week of training, the dog should be handling tracks that are fifty minutes old (the seventh day is a day of rest for both handler and dog) and be over the hump. This next week is designed to enable the handler to select the

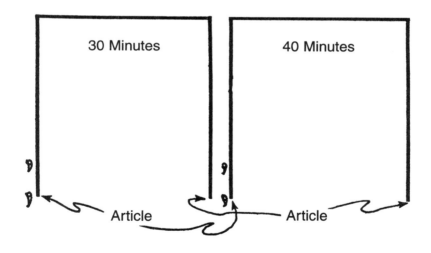

Figure 22 • **Typical Track to Approach the "Hump"**

most obvious and reliable indicators given by the dog of "loss of track – discovery of a track – following a track" that he can easily see from his position behind the dog. The dog will probably indicate these things in many different ways which can be confusing to the handler. The idea here is to select only one indicator that will reliably tell the handler what is happening without having to interpret many different indications.

As a spectator at a tracking test, you have a profile view of the dog that is tracking which is infinitely easier to read than if you were behind the dog, especially if it is a small or giant breed of dog. For example, take the Bouvier des Flandres, or especially, an all black dog. From a profile view, one can easily detect the head being raised about a foot higher than normal when the dog indicates losing the track. All the handler can see from the dog's rear is a mass of black. He cannot even see the dog's head. This indicator would be great if the handler had a profile view of the dog. Since he hasn't, he will require another more easily discerned indicator of loss of track. The same would apply to a small dog, such as a Maltese Terrier. A rise in attitude of this dog's head entails a movement of possibly less than one inch. Rather difficult for anyone to discern from thirty feet behind the dog.

These indicators can be given by the dog by changing the attitude of any part of his anatomy, including his course when on the track or his speed. Some dogs will track with their tails in repose, while others track with tails held high. Yet others will continuously wag their tails when on track. An indication by the dog of losing the track may be a change in this "tail" attitude at the moment he loses the track. For example, the dog that wags his tail when tracking may stop wagging his tail when he loses the track. Other dogs that track with tails held rigidly in repose may start to wag their tails when they lose scent of the track. No two dogs are identical in their indications. Therefore, the handler must be made aware of these changes in anatomy in order for him to function properly as part of the tracking team. By now, the handler should be aware of those indications given by the dog when actively pursuing a track. The loss and discovery indications are those which he must now learn. Some of the anatomical indicators given by dogs are listed in table form entitled "Loss of track" and "Discovery of track." These indicators are only a sample and do not even remotely encompass all of the indicators which dogs may give.

The most effective method of obtaining these reliable, observable indicators in my tracking classes is as follows. I will start to lay out a simple track with four or five right angle turns and have the entire class (with the exception of the handler) follow beside me about thirty paces off the track I'm laying. Upon arriving at the first turn, one student will remain there only thirty paces from the turn. I will instruct the remaining students to continue on another thirty paces, execute a left turn and walk parallel to my path after I've made a left turn. Following this procedure, I will drop off a student at each of the turns. Each student is asked to watch only one part of the dog's anatomy when he reaches the turn that every student has pinpointed when dropped off. They are asked to record any observable changes that occur when the dog reaches that point. When the track is completed, they are to turn the information in to me for evaluation without mentioning what they have seen to the handler. I will tell the handler which one single indicator he is to watch for as a loss and discovery sign given by the dog. By following just these examples, the handler will be able to read his dog and as time goes on, he will be able to see others, which he will use when the necessity demands it.

The tracking schedule for this eighth week is made relatively easy for the dog so that the handler will have the opportunity to read him throughout the week. The tracks should only be thirty minutes old when starting the week and should be increased in age by five minutes per day. This will make the dog's indications more subtle as time goes on and the difficulty of each track is increased with age. By the end of this eighth week, the handler should be working with his dog as a team on tracks that have been aged fifty-five minutes. Each of the tracks should vary in length from 450 to 600 paces with four to six turns included in them.

Indications

Loss of Track

Dog's Head – Normally dogs will track with their head down. When the head either comes right up all the way or part way, he has lost the track.

Dog's Tail – May be carried down and stiff while tracking. When the tail suddenly becomes erect, standing up above the dog's back, he has lost the track.

Dog's Course – Will be a straight line when on the track. Zigzagging or an erratic course or swerving to one side or the other indicates loss of track

Dog's Direction – The dog will abruptly turn 180 degrees and head toward the handler.

Track Discovery

Dog's Head – Will appear as if he snagged his nose on a hook of some sort while the body continues across the track.

Dog's Tail – May start wagging as he crosses the track and settling into a down and stiff position when he resumes the new direction.

Dog's Course – The dog will come out of his circling abruptly and move out in a straight line away from the handler, slowly at first, then pulling with a surge as his speed picks up.

Dog's Direction – The dog will search while moving at a constant speed, suddenly stopping to investigate a particular scent closely. He then changes direction, moves out slowly in a straight line until at the end of the line where he sinks into the harness and pulls.

The Tracking Schedule – Week 9

The ninth week of tracking simply consists of one track per day of regulation T.D. length each having between four and six turns. Each day increase the age of the track until the last day of the week when it should be dropped back to thirty minutes old, which the dog and handler should find easy to work. Increase the track ages as follows:

Day	Age
1	60 minutes
2	75 minutes
3	90 minutes
4	105 minutes
5	2 hours
6	30 minutes

At this time, the handler should make arrangements for certification to enter licensed competition and use the tenth week to practice under all types of conditions and ages. Both are ready for their first tracking test.

The Non-Retriever

At the beginning of this chapter, the dogs were divided into two groups, the natural retriever and the non-retriever. The only difference between these two groups of dogs is in the motivation required to get them to track. Common sense would tell you that the thrown glove represents no reason whatever for the non-retrieving dog to go out and use his nose to locate an object. The motivation we use on the non-retriever is, quite simply, food. When food is mentioned as a training aid, I often hear groans from people who have been training dogs for awhile and yet, when asked why you shouldn't use food, I seldom hear any logical answer for their disdain. I suppose if you have a natural retriever, you can easily tell others not to use it, but unfortunately there are more dogs that do not naturally retrieve than there are dogs that do retrieve. There is absolutely no reason for not employing a physical reward in the form of food. I am a firm believer that any training method that will produce the desired results short of physical pain to the dog is a valid training method.

A few years ago, an incident involving a young lady interested in training her rough Collie in tracking with a local group illustrates the difference between using the retrieve and food on a non-retriever. When the track layer attempted to get the dog interested in the glove, the dog's response was nil. The track layer then had the handler attempt to get the dog to retrieve and the dog paid no attention to the thrown glove. After many attempts that were totally fruitless, the trainer told her to go home and practice. Practice what? Throwing the glove, or holding the inattentive dog? She came to us for help and within fifteen days of training, the dog was eagerly following the track and taking the first turn. Another case involving a Bouvier des Flandres that had been taught the retrieve (inductively) resulted in the dog's expertly tracking down every frog it encountered on the track during the first few weeks of training, which utilized the glove as the motivational force. Once the dog restarted the program on the food, his interest in the frogs took second place to his interest in the track, which led to the acquisition of his T.D. title.

Dogs that are fussy eaters are no problem, but they will have to be put on a restricted diet for the duration of this training program. A type of food that is both nourishing and appetizing must be found. No two dogs are alike in this respect. Some dogs "turn on" to chicken livers, some to bacon, and most will turn on for any meat that has garlic in its makeup. It is up to the handler to determine what the dog's preference is and to institute the diet. Putting the dog on a diet can have unwanted effects if employed incorrectly. For example, a dog that has its total food consumption cut down will only be hungry until the stomach has shrunk. Then he will not feel hungry any more. When placed on a restrictive diet of 50% of his normal volume, he should be overfed on the seventh day of each week in order to cause stomach expansion, which will result in his becoming hungry once he is placed back on the diet.

Those dogs that do not possess compulsive retrieving instincts fall into one of three categories based upon their attitude to food.

---

1. The Chow Hound – the type of dog that loves to eat anything anytime

2. The Fussy Eater – is very particular about when and what he eats

3. The Finicky Eater – doesn't seem to like food at all

The first type of dog will simply obtain extra treats when tracking without being placed on a diet. The short period of time this dog food intake is increased, coupled with the physical exercise of tracking, will prevent any weight increase. The amount of food used each day on the track should equal 50% to 100% of his normal intake.

The second type of dog should be placed on a simple diet, where 50% of the dog's normal intake is earned on the track, and after completing his tracking schedule, the remaining 50% fed as a regular meal.

The third type of dog requires a total restrictive diet where no food is given as meals, and only 50% of his normal volume will be found on the track. Before each training session, proportion the food drops in accordance with the NON-RETRIEVER schedule in Figure 23. The largest drop should be located at the end of each track and should be twice the size of any other food drop. Proceed to train the dog as described in this chapter without using any articles until the first turn is instituted at the beginning of the third week of training. At that point, fill the glove with the last drop, and when he discovers it, encourage him to pick it up. Should he refuse to pick it up, the handler is to go up to the find and help the dog get some food out of it and then throw it a short distance, while encouraging the dog to get it. You want to make the dog believe that the only way he can get the food out of the article is by bringing it back to you so that you can help him get it out.

The dog will indicate when it is time to discontinue the use of food by refusing the smaller drops in his hurry to find the last food drop, which he knows to be the largest. This normally occurs between the third and fifth week of training. Once the third week of training has begun, and the first turn incorporated, the food drops are reduced to one food drop in the middle of each leg and the largest in the article. When the dog is refusing some of the food drops in order to reach the end of the track where the largest prize is waiting, start to eliminate one food drop per day. At the end of the fifth week of training, stop placing the food in the article and carry it on your person so that you can reward him for his finding the glove.

The "Non-Retriever"
Use some nourishing food that the dog really loves.

Day	Distance of food drop from the previous food group								
	No.1	No.2	No.3	No.4	No.5	No.6	No.7	No.8	No. 9
1	10	10	10	10	10	10	10	10	10
2	10	10	10	10	10	10	10	10	10
3	10	15	20	25	30	35	40	45	50
4	10	15	20	25	30	35	40	45	50
5	15	25	35	45	55	65	75	85	95
6	25	35	45	55	65	75	85	95	100
8	35	45	55	65	75	85	95	100	100
9	35	45	55	65	75	85	95	100	100
10	35	45	55	65	75	85	95	100	100
11	35	45	55	65	75	85	95	100	100
12	35	45	55	65	75	85	95	100	100
13	35	45	55	65	75	85	95	100	100
14	35	45	55	65	75	85	95	100	100

Once corners have commenced, one food drop in the middle of each leg.

Third lesson: Stuff glove with food.

Normal feed resumes after two weeks, only if the dog is passing up food drops and appears well-motivated. If not, maintain diet until fourth week when normal feeding should be instituted.

If the dog is not a Chow Hound, use the restrictive diet mentioned.

Should a dog started on the retrieve prove to have motivational problems, he should be switched over to the food drop scheduled here without changing his regular track design. This means the dog may be on the third day of the third week track design while using the first day food drop schedule.

The Food Drop Schedule

The food drop schedule illustrated here signifies the distance from the start where the first food drop is placed and the distance between each drop, bearing in mind that regardless of the schedule, the largest drop occurs at the end of each track. The actual track design for the first five days is illustrated next, showing the food drops as they occur along the track. The distances shown are from the starting flag but are the same distance apart as depicted in the food drop schedule.

In order to properly utilize both the track design and the food drop schedule, I recommend that handlers draw out each day's track design, marking the distances from the starting flag where each food drop is to be located.

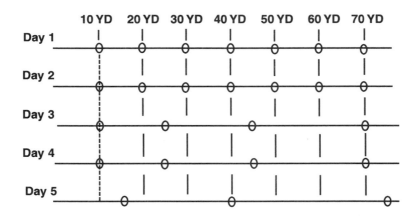

Figure 23 • **Food Drop Design for Non-Retrievers**

Examination of the food drop schedule will show where the food should be dropped each day of the tracking program. For example, on the first day, when the track is only twenty yards long, there will be a food drop at the ten yard mark, as well as at the twenty yard mark. On the fifth day of tracking, when the track is eighty yards long, there will be a food drop at the fifteen yard, forty yard, seventy-five yard and at the eighty yard mark. Regardless of where the food drops are located, there will always be the largest drop at the end of the track as per the food drop design on the last page.

I have often been asked why I use these stipulated distances and to be perfectly honest, it is simply because at these distances it works. I have tried other food drop distances without any positive results. When I return to these distances, it has always worked. I have no idea why. As long as I can keep getting the results with these distances, I shall continue to use them.

Quite often, on the first day, I have looked at dogs that appeared as if they had the retrieving instinct, only to discover a few weeks later that it wasn't a natural instinct, but a trained response. The dog had been trained to retrieve during obedience training. Without exception, we have run into problems that necessitated the restarting of these dogs, using food and we then had no problems. It doesn't matter whether the dog was trained to retrieve through force or inductively. It is a false reaction that must be critically judged when starting dogs into this program.

Those individuals who are categorized as having non-retrievers seem to be disappointed upon this discovery, especially when they are told that their dogs are starting on food. These dogs have, more often than not, been the first dogs to show positive results and have been the first dogs in our classes to obtain their tracking titles. If it weren't so much work in preparing the food beforehand and having to pinpoint the food drops before laying the tracks, I think I would prefer starting all dogs with food.

Once the dogs (non-retrievers, as well as retrievers) have obtained their T.D. or when they have completed this ten-week session, they are ready for the more advanced work in TDX.

Ilene Newman, the first handler in North America
with two TDX dogs, *Sheba* and *Mike*.

TDX Training Methods 5

During the tenth week of tracking training the handler has his two positive indicators to watch for when handling his dog on tracks that are becoming older. It is now up to the handler to start observing his dog for other signs that something has happened on the track. By now, the handler should be able to feel the difference in tautness on the tracking line a moment or two before he can recognize a visual indicator. Don't be fooled by a dog that normally tracks at a steady pace and suddenly surges forward at a run, pulling hard with his head up, especially in a new direction. He might have spotted a bird or scented a rabbit. The behavior of a trained dog when on a track is fairly constant and a sudden deviation from this behavior could mean something other than a track.

The handler must learn to expect slight changes in tracking behavior when one of the many variables affecting the track scent strength changes. The tendency to overshoot is greater when the wind is blowing in the same direction as the dog is tracking and should be handled with more tension on the tracking line. When tracking in areas of little vegetation or hard clay, the handler should ease up on the tension to encourage the dog to move on what little scent might be available. When the dog has indicated loss of track in an area with little vegetation, allow him more line to explore areas of vegetation that border on the sparse area. He just might be able to better discover the track's presence should it run in that direction.

The demands of a TDX track are enormous. Many dogs never even reach the first turn. The proper start is of critical importance and the dog must take sufficient starting scent. Secondly, stamina must be built up in the TDX trainee. In many cases, I have seen dogs work well up to 800 to 1,000 yards, at which point they simply quit tracking. Probably the greatest reason for failure of so many TDX hopefuls are the cross tracks which are more than one hour fresher. In the training of a TDX dog these are just some of the critical areas that he must be prepared for if he is to pass the TDX test consistently.

At one TDX test, I can recall a German Shepherd that performed an excellent job of tracking up to the second glove. When the handler attempted to restart the dog, it refused. It was tired and had enough. This was a classical case of a dog that just wasn't prepared for the distances demanded by TDX. The rules state a minimum of 1,000 yards, but there is no maximum. At another TDX test, the track was started at one concession road and headed for the next concession road, which was, unknown to the judge, one mile away. The track had to cross a road and that road was one mile away; however, there were several turns before that road was reached. The dog did an excellent job of tracking and successfully completed the track, over one mile in length. Obviously, this dog had been properly prepared for this sort of a demand.

When we start training a dog and handler for TDX, we try to change one variable at a time, while keeping the other variables constant. These other variables are not important, so we attempt to reduce the difficulty they may present. We are primarily interested in increasing the stamina of a dog. This means training him to track a very long distance. We just ensure that there are few other difficulties facing him during this week of training. The dog should be capable of tracking 600 yards on a track that is two hours old, with only four turns in the track and one article at the end. From this point, the strain of performing on a TDX type of track will certainly have an effect on the dog's performance. To ensure that the dog will not lose enthusiasm for tracking, we have to let him have a day's break in between tracking assignments. Following this one day break, we are going to put him on a very simple, short distance, fresh track that he can follow with great ease without tiring. This second track we call the "motivational" track. We give the dog another day's rest and then hit him with another TDX assignment that will task his abilities. Throughout this TDX program we will be using this technique of a hard track followed by an easy one, and then back to the tough tracking again.

During the first week of TDX tracking, we do not give the dog this break for the simple reason that we want to see if we can find his breaking point when it comes to a long distance track. The ratio of turns per yardage of track is held to about one turn per 250 yards.

TDX Training Schedule – Week 1

Each day of tracking during this first week's assignment uses only one article at the track's conclusion. This means the dog has to track for a long period of time before reaching the glove. For the steady but fast moving dog that doesn't waste any time, it will mean that he'll have to track for about thirty minutes to reach the 3,000-yard mark. The length of the track is increased in large steps to 3,000 yards with the age remaining at one hour. On the fifth day, we increase the track age to 1.5 hours, while the track remains at 3,000 yards. Should the dog stop tracking when engaged on these long tracks, the handler should double check the distance the dog has managed to work successfully. For the next several days the track should be increased by 100 yard increments in order to get across to the dog that the article is only a short distance further. Most dogs that have been trained under the heavy tracking load of the TD portion of this program have little problem with these extended tracks. In many cases, where the dog was on three tracks per day, he was performing over 1,000 yards per day.

At the end of this first week of TDX training, the length of the tracks is to be reduced to 1500 yards and the number of turns maintained at no less than six nor any more than eight.

Stamina Increase

Day	Track Length	Numbers of Corners	Track Age
1	800 Yards	3	1 hr
2	1600 Yards	6	1 hr
3	2000 Yards	8	1 hr
4	3000 Yards	12	1 hr
5	3000 Yards	12	1.5 hr

Number of Articles – 1
Terrain – Varying Types of Vegetation

TDX Training Schedule – Week 2

Two variables become the target of the second week of TDX training. Track age is to be systematically increased, while we teach handler and dog how to start on a track that has only one starting flag. The dog is to track every other day and the second track will be the motivational track already mentioned.

In TDX tests, as well as Schutzhund tracking, only one starting stake is used to identify the point where the track layer started. From this point, he could have traveled in any direction to his handler. More than five yards in the wrong direction by the handler could result in hearing the disqualification whistle. This problem necessitates the implementation of correct training practices right at the start.

The track layer must inform the handler of the track's

initial direction during this week, so that the handler may approach the start of the track at a ninety degree angle. The handler is to place the dog in a *down* position with his head over the trampled area, close to the stake, but facing across the track, rather than in the direction of the track, as in Figure 24. Use the same method to start him tracking as in the previous training, only watch the dog's behavior closely. Should he have

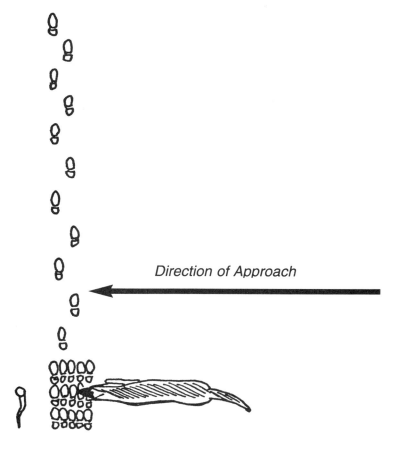

Figure 24 • **Single Flag Technique**

the tendency to start off in the direction he is facing, do not move. Most dogs will do this at this point, since the track has always been out in front of them before. Encourage him to search for the track and permit him to search in his own manner. Do not give him any guidance. Continue to face the direction the dog was facing when lying down until he discovers the track's correct direction and has moved out in a straight line until the knot has passed through the left hand. At this point, the handler should begin to follow – using an increased tension on the line until the dog sinks into the harness and is pulling with certainty.

Once the dog has been placed in a *down* position, he should remain there for at least ten seconds before starting. Starting scent is of critical importance should he lose the track at any point. Dogs that have not taken adequate starting scent from the beginning seem to forget what the scent is like that they are looking for, once they have lost the track for any length of time. The will overshoot a turn with the wind blowing from behind and then, when they cast over the actual track, they seem to give no recognition to the track they are crossing. On the other hand, those dogs that have taken scent well at the start do not have this problem. I can remember one TDX dog that overran a turn and circled wide around his handler. He scented right up to within a foot of the track, lifted his head to exhale while taking a few more steps, causing him to pass over the track and then began scenting for the track again. He performed the same way again and again. For twenty minutes the dog circled and always lifted his head as he approached the new direction of the track. At the end of the twenty minutes, he took the extra step while scenting, discovered the track and completed it successfully.

This ability of the dog to retain the memory of a given scent is utilized later when teaching him scent strength discrimination in crosstrack training. In order to discriminate properly, however, he must have taken adequate scent at the beginning of the track or he may take the crosstrack without realizing it.

Training Schedule

Track	Length	Turns	Articles	Age
1	1500 Yards	6	1	1.5 hr.
2	400 Yards	3	1	0.5 hr.
3	1500 Yards	6	1	2.0 hr.

By the end of the second week of TDX training, the dog will be looking for the start of the track's direction and its age will be back up to two hours old. He'll probably believe at this time that the tracking is all over once he has located the object of his search. The time has come to teach him that the track will continue after finding an article and this is the purpose of the third week.

TDX Training Schedule – Week 3

The dog that will retrieve the article is an asset in TDX and will present less of a problem when it comes to restarting him once he has located an article. From the beginning of tracking training you should have been dropping to one knee and coaxing the dog to return to you with the article that he has found. In restarting the dog, we use this same technique to great advantage. Once he has discovered the article, we know for certain the exact location of the track, as well as its direction from us. Having taken the article from the dog and placed it out of his sight (in a pocket), we can restart the dog in the same direction where he first located it. The track between the dog and where he located the article has not been fouled by the handler walking over the track. We know that, according to the rules of TDX competition, there can be no crosstrack within ten yards of an article, nor can there be a turn. When the dog heads back out on the track between the handler and the article's location, he should be able to pick up the track easily and should be able to move out another ten yards with no other problems facing him.

In this manner, it is as if we were tracking another TD type of track to the next article. Our start is where we receive the article and the second flag indicating direction is the location of the find. When the find is actually made, the handler should come to a halt and, with a quick snap, throw the tracking line out to one side so as not to interfere with the dog. He should drop to one knee and call the dog to retrieve it, praise the dog enthusiastically for bringing it back, place the article out of sight, stand up and command him to resume his tracking. Should the dog act as if he is finished, step out in the direction of the track and encourage him to find it.

The non-retriever that simply indicates the article's presence requires that the handler go up to him, retrieve the glove himself and restart the dog from that point, only there are only ten paces left that haven't been fouled where no turn or crosstrack should exist. One other problem that can develop when handling a non-retriever is the method of indication and for how long it is indicated. One handler – dog team was almost at the end of a well done TDX track when the handler noticed poison ivy in the area where the track was heading and having had a bad experience with this weeks before, looked for a place to walk through it. The handler took her eyes off the dog for several seconds, just as the dog came to a halt, indicating the last article on the track, but the handler hadn't noticed the indication while navigating her way through the poison ivy. The dog waited for only a moment, then proceeded to track the track layer out of the field, which resulted in the harsh sound of the whistle.

In order to teach the dog restarts, use a simple track of about 400 yards length as depicted in Figure 25 for one day. Deposit two articles on each long leg of the track for a total of six articles and let the track age only thirty minutes before starting the dog. Always give the dog about a ten to twenty second break after putting the article out of sight. This will get his mind off that article before restarting him on the track. The following day place him in the training schedule.

Training Schedule

Track	Length	Turns	Articles	Age
1	1500 Yards	6-8	6	2 1/4 hr
2	400 Yards	3	1	0.5 hr
3	1500 Yards	6-8	6	2.5 hr

* Note – On the Days That the Dog is Normally Resting, Run the Restart Track Design.

At the conclusion of the third week of TDX training, the dog should be tracking a 1500 yard track, two and one-half hours old, that has six articles dropped on it. He is now ready for the next problem area, "Roads."

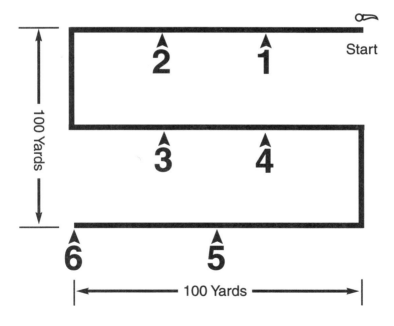

Figure 25 • **Restarting Track Design**

By dropping to one knee to receive the retrieve, the handler
now has established where the track is
and its direction, without fouling the track.

TDX Training Schedule – Week 4

The Canadian TDX rules call for the track to cross a road
at some point. The roads that have been selected have been
well-traveled, paved highways rather than the single lane farm
roads that would only permit one vehicle at a time, weather permitting. Small roads pose little problem to an experienced dog
with a little training, but the wide highway with steep irrigation
ditches on either side require expert handling on the part of the
handler, as well as the dog. I have heard stories about the proficiency of dogs when tracking on a paved surface, all of which
were second hand. I have never seen a dog demonstrate even
mediocre proficiency on pavement myself. Some of these dogs
that were supposed to be proficient trackers on pavement could
not successfully handle a thirty-minute-old track in a well-vegetated area, which leaves me doubtful to say the least. Trailing
dogs, or dogs that work by detecting airborne scent immediately
after a person has passed through a paved area would probably
detect those individuals, but not by following a track. Even the
best TDX dogs that I have known could not demonstrate any
degree of proficiency on pavement. Since the TDX track that
must be followed is more than three hours old, I assume that the

dog is not going to pick up the track when on the paved road, and it is not necessary that he be able to. All that is required is that the dog cross the road and pick up the track on the other side.

When training the dog on roads, we teach him that the track will continue on the other side of the road and that when he arrives at a road to simply raise his head, cross to the other side, pick up the track and continue his normal tracking. When the handler sees that the dog is approaching a road, he should increase his own pace, move up the tracking line until he is only about ten feet behind the dog, slack off the tension, and while the dog crosses the road, get across himself. When approaching the road, the handler should pick out a spot immediately on the other side where it appears that the track is heading so that he will cross to that point, regardless of where the dog crosses to. Once on the other side, the handler should remain stationary while the dog searches for and resumes the track. When moving up the line to the ten foot mark, the handler should look to see if there is a deep ditch, low fence or other physical obstacle and, if necessary, drop the line in order to get through himself, while the dog picks his own way through the obstacle. Dogs will sometimes have the tendency to cross a road at an angle, rather than in the direction that the track was heading. This makes it necessary for the handler to keep his perspective and ensure that he will be at the approximate site of the track once across.

The ideal training area for roads is one where several industries are located that have vegetated areas between their plants and the main road. Lay a single leg track between their buildings and the main road crossing their driveways as the track is being laid. Cross at least four to six driveways in a 300 yard track and deposit an article twenty paces after crossing the driveway. Start the dog on the track as soon as it is laid. By the time he has crossed the first few driveways, he'll have the message and be lifting his head while running across the remaining roads. When following the tracking schedule for this week, the track layer should lay the assigned track as detailed in the schedule. While this track is aging, lay the track I have just

*The handler moves up to about ten feet behind the dog
that is approaching a road, slackening the line
to allow the dog to cross the road.*

described. The dog should track the single leg track immediately before going on to the assigned track called for in the schedule below.

Training Schedule

Track	Length	Turns	Articles	Age	Roads
1	1500 Yards	6-8	6	2 3/4 hr.	1 Narrow
2	400 Yards	3	1	0.5 hr.	None
3	1500 Yards	6-8	6	2.5 hr.	1 Wide

At the end of this week, the dog should be performing the entire TDX track with the exception of the crosstracks. His performance on these aged tracks will still not be really efficient nor is it expected to be, at this point. The motivational tracks he should perform well on, but the age will undoubtedly be a stumbling block at this point. The handler should not worry too much about this, for he is about to start all over again, going from a relatively fresh track all the way back up to the three hour plus mark. The next big problem area he has to master, along with the handler, are the crosstracks.

TDX Training Schedule – Week 5

About ten years before writing this book, I would have said that there were two areas of difficulty that contributed to the failure of most TDX competitors, the age of the track (many dogs couldn't even get started) and the crosstracks. These problems are still there, but their order has definitely changed with the crosstracks taking over first place. The general consensus among trainers of considerable experience was that it was by sheer luck that a dog managed to get past the crosstracks successfully. If the dog did notice the fresher crosstrack, then he would most certainly take it. I disagreed with that opinion on the basis that a dog could be taught scent discrimination between two tracks, just as they are taught scent discrimination of articles in Utility. Today I have to agree with that opinion, but only if the conditions are just right.

The experiments I conducted with two different track layers on the 'X" pattern (described in Chapter II) showed that the dog could, in fact, tell the difference between two tracks that were laid by two different track layers as long as there was a great weight differential on tracks over two hours in age. Should the weight of the two track layers be equal, then the dogs could tell the difference between the two tracks when fresh, but not when they were over two hours old. Further observation of the behavior of dogs trained to differentiate crosstracks showed that they had the tendency to check out a crosstrack for a much longer distance when the weights of the two different track layers were becoming close to the same.

Some dogs could distinguish the difference between weights of ten pounds, but this was the exception, not the rule. This pointed to the necessity of "luck" when the track layer and the crosstrack layer weighed the same should the dog pick up the crosstrack. If lucky, in this case, the dog just might overrun the crosstrack and not even notice it.

Another factor contributing to the dog's taking the crosstrack was the angle at which the crosstrack intersected the track and the wind direction at the time the dog arrived at the intersection. We found that the closer the crosstrack came to paralleling the actual track, the greater the tendency of the dog to take the crosstrack. This was especially true if the wind was blowing in the right direction at the time the dog arrived at the intersection of the two tracks. Should the dog be tracking slightly downwind of the track at the time of arrival at the intersection, he would readily swing off onto the crosstrack if the angle was slight as depicted in Figure 26.

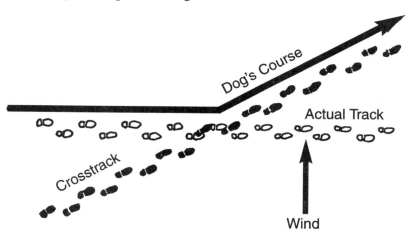

The dog following a track, slightly on the downwind side, will reach the intersection of the crosstrack and take the crosstrack if the crosstrack is laid almost parallel to the actual track.

Figure 26 • **Angular Crosstrack**

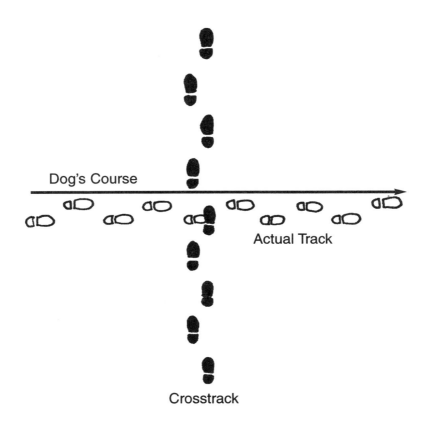

Dog's Course

Actual Track

Crosstrack

The right angle crosstrack presents
the least problem to the dog.

Figure 27 • **Right Angle Crosstrack**

The chances of a dog not even noticing the crosstrack would probably be the greatest if the crosstrack layer intersected the track at a right angle without actually stepping on the track. The dog, moving at a fairly good speed, possibly line tracking at the moment he passed between the crosstrack layer's footprints would continue on the track with no indication of the existence of a crosstrack at that point. Should the crosstrack layer actually step on the track, and should the dog be scenting at the time he arrives at the intersection, he'll probably notice the crosstrack, especially if the weights of the two track layers are substantially different. When this does occur, the dog that isn't trained on scent strength discrimination will probably stop to investigate and commit himself to the fresher track. The dog that has received training in scent strength discrimination will check out the crosstrack, first in one direction, then in the other direction, realize that it isn't the track he started on and refuse to take it. This type of recognition and crosstrack identification is what the handler is striving for during this phase of training.

Before starting training, the handler should realize what the end result is to be, as well as the process by which he is to attain this result. The age of the track, as stipulated by the regulations, is at least three hours old. The crosstrack is to be laid one hour after the completion of the track itself. Since the distance of the track is to be 1,000 yards minimum, which takes about thirty minutes to lay, the difference between these two tracks is one hour and thirty minutes. This means that the crosstracks are going to average ninety minutes fresher than the track. The important aspect of crosstrack training is to get the dog to discriminate between the relative scent strengths of two tracks that are ninety minutes apart and both beyond the hump. The track layers selected for the laying of the track and crosstrack should be substantially different in weight.

During this training, the handler must realize that when the dog is tracking, there is a very good chance to have inadvertent crosstracks laid by individuals who are unaware of the fact that a dog is in training. Since the dog cannot distinguish between individuals who are close in weight, there is also a good chance that the dog will commit himself to their track when the handler believes no other crosstrack exists. Improper handling of the dog when this occurs can result in a dog that will refuse to continue tracking. The first rule the handler must burn into his memory is that the dog is never to be scolded when he commits himself to a crosstrack, or he will be causing this phenomena to occur.

My first attempts at crosstrack training included the verbal chastisement of a dog that erroneously committed himself to a crosstrack, whether in training or inadvertently. The results became obvious quickly thereafter. It took longer and longer to get the dog to resume tracking on the correct track. At one point the dog had to be walked through more than 500 yards of track before he resumed tracking. This behavior was rather frightening, to say the least, until close examination showed what was happening. When the dog found a crosstrack that was freshly laid by a person of equal weight, he actually believed that the crosstrack was the original track he was following. By berating the dog for this action, he would refuse to go with the original track since it possessed the same scent and I had already scolded him for attempting to follow it. Each time he was scolded for his actions, it would take longer and longer for me to convince him that the scent of the track I was walking him on was in fact the one to follow and that he would not be scolded for going with it. By altering the method of handling when the dog committed such an error, I was able to complete his training with no further problems of this sort nor with any other dogs as well.

Should the dog ever take a known crosstrack or an inadvertent crosstrack in training, the handler should watch closely for commitment by the dog. At that moment, call the dog in an excited tone to "look what I found" to break the dog's attention from the crosstrack. Take several steps to get him past the crosstrack and allow him to search out the track's presence at that point. In this manner, the dog hasn't received chastisement for doing what may have seemed, to him, the thing to do.

By laying a track with a crosstrack or two on it and expecting a dog to learn discrimination of the two would be like taking a dog for a one mile walk, insisting that he *sit* twice when the handler came to a halt twice and expecting the dog to learn to sit automatically at every halt. Any person who has trained a dog in obedience knows that this expectation is ludicrous. In order to teach a dog scent strength discrimination properly requires that he work through many crosstracks each day of his training. Before we can expect him to learn discrimination between such subtle differences in scent, we must first teach him to discriminate between two track scents that will be obvious to him. Then we must work toward the more subtle differences.

The track design shown in Figure 28 has a total of sixteen crosstracks of different angles from right angles, to slightly angular, to extreme angles. It will present the dog and handler with sixteen different types of crosstracks. Wind direction is not a criteria, since the dog will be hitting the crosstracks at all angles with respect to the wind. Since we are operating with relatively short tracks that are not aged like a TDX track, we are not concerned with breaking the dog every other day for a rest. The dog is to track every day. By altering the age of the track and the crosstrack, as per the tracking schedule, we are also altering the time differential between the track and crosstrack to get the ninety-minute differential we are after.

Training Schedule

Day	Crosstrack Laid At:	Dog Start	Track Age	Crosstrack Age	Scent Strength Different
1	30 Min.	1 hr.	1 hr.	30 Min.	30 Min.
2	45 Min.	1 1/2 hr.	1 1/2 hr.	45 Min.	45 Min.
3	60 Min.	2 hr.	2 hr.	1 hr.	1 hr.
4	60 Min.	2 1/4 hr.	2 1/4 hr.	1 1/4 hr.	1 1/4 hr.
5	1 1/4 Hr.	2 1/2 hr.	2 1/2 hr.	1 1/4 hr.	1 1/4 hr.
6	1 1/2 Hr.	3 hr.	3 hr.	1 1/2 hr.	1 1/2 hr.

The track layer lays the 860 yard track as detailed and, while laying the track has the crosstrack layer follow beside him twenty paces off the track. After proceeding twenty paces from the start, the crosstrack layer is to place a stake in the ground and continue to walk alongside the track layer. After proceeding another forty paces, the crosstrack layer is to place a second stake in the ground and then again one hundred twenty paces later a third stake is to be placed in the ground. When the track layer reaches the turn, the crosstrack layer is to continue another fifty paces beyond the turn, execute a right turn and proceed an additional one hundred paces and wait for the track layer to complete the track up to the sixth turn. While laying the track, articles should only be deposited on the twenty-yard legs in order to keep them away from a crosstrack. When the track layer has made the sixth turn, the crosstrack layer is to proceed once more alongside the track layer, but about twenty paces from the actual track. When the track layer has gone twenty paces from the last turn the crosstrack layer is to place a fourth stake in the ground and again place a stake in the ground one hundred sixty paces later. At the scheduled time for the crosstrack to be laid, the crosstack layer should approach the first stake, ensuring that he is at least twenty paces from the actual track and then proceed to walk from stake to stake as per the crosstrack training design.

The stakes are left in the ground, so that the handler will know should the dog commit himself to taking a crosstrack. In this way, he can respond as mentioned earlier. The dog that manages to complete the track without even indicating a crosstrack is not a dog that is successful, for it simply means that he didn't notice their presence and the effort has been wasted as far as crosstrack training is concerned. Those crosstracks noticed, or even taken, are the ones that can be considered successful in terms of training. Should the dog take a crosstrack, be sure to give him time to investigate it. If total commitment by the dog is obvious, simply distract the dog verbally (not with a jerk on the line or a verbal berating) and take a few steps past the point where the crosstrack is known to be.

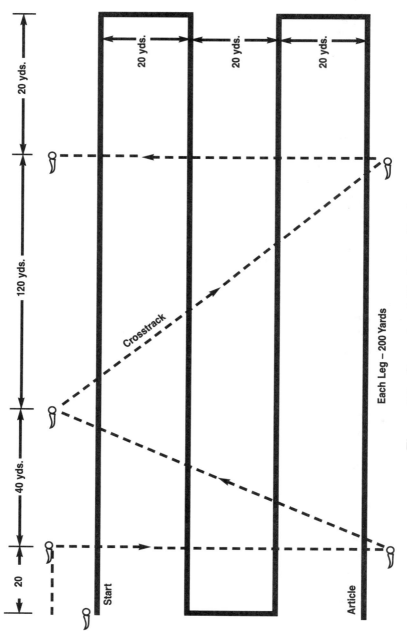

Figure 28 • **Crosstrack Training Design**

20 yds.

20 yds.

20 yds.

20 yds.

120 yds.

40 yds.

20

Crosstrack

Each Leg – 200 Yards

Start

Article

Tracking Dog Theory & Methods

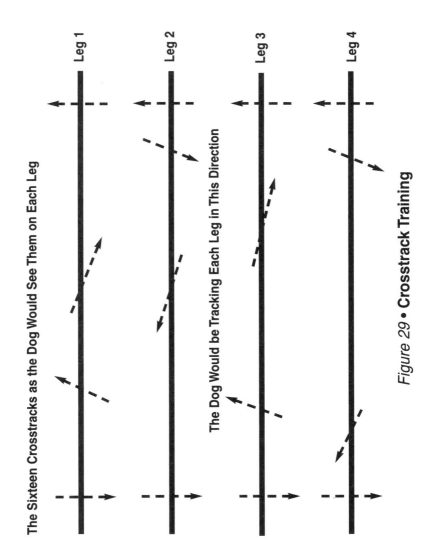

Figure 29 • **Crosstrack Training**

The end of this week of training will have seen the dog and handler through an increased track age and time differential on a saturation of crosstracks until the age of both crosstracks and track are up to TDX standards. Both are now ready for the final phase of TDX training before entering a licensed TDX test.

TDX Training Schedule – Week 6

In order to prepare the dog for the rigors of a TDX test from this point on and maintain the crosstrack training, the dog is placed on a schedule that calls for two tracks per day when employing the TDX track and a day of rest, followed by a motivational track that the dog and handler will find extremely easy to complete. The two track of TDX nature will include a "starter" track for crosstracks, plus a regulation TDX track of approximately 1500 paces, three to three and one-half hours old that crosses a road and has two crosstracks at widely-spaced intervals.

The "starter" track is simply a single leg that is 100 to 150 yards long that has one article at the end and four crosstracks of differing angles on it. The track layer is to lay the starter track first before proceeding to lay a regulation TDX track, return to direct the cross track layer on the starter track and, finally, to direct the crosstrack layer where to lay the crosstracks on the regular TDX track. Care should be exercised to ensure that the crosstracks are laid at the correct time by the crosstrack layer and that he continues past the point of intersection by an additional twenty-five paces. The starter track design is included in Figure 30. The number of articles should be reduced to three and the Track layer should endeavor to lay the track through areas of rough terrain, underbrush and any other areas that may present the handler and his dog with difficulty.
During this phase, the handler should attempt to increase his expertise at handling the dog through areas of difficulty as described here.

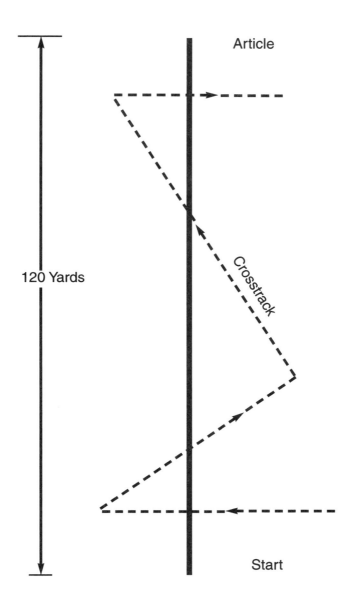

120 Yards

Article

Crosstrack

Start

Figure 30 • **TDX Starter Track**

Underbrush

When the handler can see the possibility of the track going through a section of underbrush, he should move up on the tracking line to the ten foot mark so that he can see how difficult the area is to get through. Should the dog enter such an area where the handler cannot get through. Then the handler should drop the line, seek an avenue that he can manage and, as quickly as possible, pick up the line to pull it through so that the task of the handler is to see that nothing interrupts his dog's concentration while tracking.

Searching in an Area of Trees

Should the dog indicate a turn in an area of tree growth and take the line around a tree when circling, the handler should make a mental note of the spot he is standing on, where he knows the track to be. He should then quickly walk up to the tree, seize the line at that point and, while stepping back to the spot he left, pull the line around the tree without interrupting the dog's search for the track's new direction.

Searching in Sparsely Vegetated Area

On occasion there will be a turn made in an area with little or no vegetation. In this type of situation, it is wise to have the fifty foot line mentioned in Chapter III. You have been tracking the dog at the thirty foot mark and have been moving up the line to the ten foot mark when an obstacle is seen coming up ahead. At this point, when the dog is searching out sparsely vegetated area, the handler should allow the dog more line, when it is obvious that an adjacent area within reach of the fifty foot line contains more vegetation where the dog may pick up the track more easily. In this manner, the handler is helping the dog by making available to him a wider and possibly more effective searching area.

TDX Training Schedule – Week 7

Up to this point in the dog's training, he is probably line tracking. This enables him to conserve energy and is effective as long as the dog is not moving at a flat out gallop that can

---

                                              Tracking Dog Theory & Methods

result in his badly overshooting a turn. When he arrives at an area of little vegetation or a plowed field, he will have a "step track" since the only place that will carry any scent is where the track layer actually stepped. Most line tracking dogs will run into severe difficulty at this point when they first hit it, even those dogs that track extremely well on tracks that are four or more hours old. During this week it is up to the handler to prepare his dog for this eventuality.

Select an area where there is both a vegetated area and a place devoid of vegetation, such as a plowed field. The track layer should begin the track in the vegetated area, making two or three turns before cutting the corner of the plowed field. The initial distance of penetration into the plowed field should be short, in the neighborhood of several paces only and doubling it each day. When the dog enters the plowed area, or any area devoid of vegetation and runs into difficulty, don't wait. You should reach out and touch a footprint and excitedly call the dog's attention to it. Move slowly one step at a time while encouraging the dog until he is picking out each print by himself and is starting to move out on his own. It will become obvious when he starts to sniff out each print ahead of you, seeming to quarter with his nose virtually bouncing off the edges of the footprints. Once you have him step tracking, you're ready at last for an attempt at TDX and all the suspenseful loneliness it brings as you wait for the track to "cool off" at a TDX test.

Classical Problem Solving 6

Unfortunately no two dogs or handlers are exactly alike. If they were, we would still have discrepancies in the way each dog was handled during his training. Differences in temperament, character, personalities and attention spans may result in problems that develop during training. When a problem is detected by the handler, it should be identified and corrected before it becomes an unwanted, but conditioned behavior that will interfere with the dog's progress. It only stands to reason that not every dog possesses those dynamic traits that would make him a natural dog for tracking training. Every dog can, in fact, learn to track and to surmount those problems that may develop if the correct action is taken at the right time.

Most problems that develop during tracking training are what I call classical in nature, that is to say, they are a group of problems, few in number, but commonly encountered by those trainers interested in tracking training. Some of these problems prevent many dogs from obtaining their titles and frustrate their handlers because the solution to them is unknown. Some problems are the result of improper training procedures, while others are simply a matter of a lack of training on the part of the

---

handler. I have watched dogs track that have received years of training and when asked where I would place these dogs in my training program, I've had to answer "at the beginning of the second week."

This chapter deals with these classic problems, first as an observable behavior that is obviously unwanted, and then the process by which the problem can be corrected. The methods of correction are those employed by myself and advocated to my students when the problem is identified and which have resulted in most cases with correction of the unwanted behavior.

Problem: *The dog has been tracking well up to three turns on tracks that are twenty minutes old when, abruptly, he stopped tracking. He seems to have no interest in even trying to find the track and simply wanders around looking for something else to do.*

Solution: Should the problem persist for a few days, then it is obvious that he has lost interest and requires remotivation. About one dog in five seems to undergo this phase and it only requires a series of motivational tracks to bring this dog right back up to the same level of proficiency that he had before entering this phase. This series of five simple tracks laid and executed one after the other will remotivate the dog to start tracking again. I have often been asked the reason why it has such a profound effect on the dog, and I have to honestly answer that I really don't know why. The design and techniques evolved over the years and have proven so successful that I simply use them without questioning why.

The track layer is to lay five tracks as depicted in the manner stated on the design. The first track is about 250 yards long with two turns and single laid. The second track has only one turn, is 150 yards long, and is double laid. The third track is also 150 yards long, and is double laid. The third track is also 150 yards long, has one turn, and is double laid with the exception of the turn. For ten paces past the turn, before double laying the entire track, it is to be triple laid. Both of the next tracks have no turns, are 100 yards long, and the dog is to be at the start of the last track when it is laid. While laying this last track, the track layer should behave in the same manner with the article as on the first day of this training program. Once the tracks are completed, the dog is to be started on the last track laid and continue to track each one in the reverse order they were laid. By the time the dog gets to the last track, it will have aged to about twenty to twenty-five minutes, and he'll be back at par.

If the dog was a non-retriever at the start of the program, food should be used in place of the article, except on the first track laid, which should have the article containing food.

Problem: *The dog is normally an excellent tracking dog capable of tracking a regulation TD track. Occasionally, he stops tracking totally and seems unable to pick up the track in an area where he normally tracks well.*

Solution: There is no one single reason for a dog to stop tracking. Many different things could be causing this problem. What you have to do is to sit down and ask yourself what has happened in the few days preceding his cessation of tracking that is not a normal occurrence. For example, has any medication been administered to the dog? Has he gone off his food?

One dog of mine several years ago performed in this same manner only a week before entering his first TDX test. In an area where he normally tracked well on three to four hour old tracks, he couldn't seem to find the track, although he looked for it in a sluggish manner. There was no improvement in the next day or so. I sat down and asked myself what had happened in the past few days preceding the problem? The dog had come down with eczema and was placed on oral administration of cortisone. Enquiries with veterinarians indicated there may be side effects, such as lethargy, but none that would affect his olfactory system that they knew about. I insisted that the oral administration of cortisone cease anyway. They placed him on a cortisone spray instead. Three days later he was back to his old self, tracking three to four hour old tracks with no difficulty.

All drugs and medications will have some side effects. Which of these side effects will reduce olfactory powers, concentration, or any characteristic necessary for the dog to properly work a track is as yet unknown. *Caracide*, used in the prevention of heartworm, seems to affect most dogs for about two weeks after it has been administered for the first time. After two weeks it seems to have no detrimental effect that can be observed when tracking.

Problem: *The dog follows the initial tracks in training, but seems to be quartering a great deal on the downwind side of the track.*

Solution: There is a good chance that the dog is either trailing or fringe following. This must be stopped before it becomes a habit that is very difficult to break. The cause could be one of several things.

1. The tracks laid at the beginning of the program must run directly into or with the wind. A crosswind occurring often at this stage will contribute greatly to this problem.

2. Insufficient tension on the tracking line will result in this quartering type of behavior.

3. There may be so much scent present that the dog with an exceptionally good nose can pick it up further downwind of the track.
    Depending on which one of these possible causes it was, the remedies are as follows:

1. Repeat the first two weeks, ensuring that the track does run into or with the wind as directed by the tracking schedule.

2. Increase the tension on the line to get the dog pulling. This behavior can be seen more often in dogs that are attempting to track off lead and can be corrected easily by making them pull.

3. Increase the age of the tracks by fifteen minutes to lessen the available scent.

Should it be impossible to determine which of the above is at fault, then employ all three techniques simultaneously.

Problem: *While tracking, the dog acts as if he has lost the scent of the track and is unable to pick it up again.*

Solution: It is possible that, while tracking, the hump has been reached, which will cause this phenomenon. Ensure that you know exactly where the track is before attempting to restart the dog. Hold onto the back strap of the harness, point directly at the track, and, while walking in the direction of the track, point to the track. With great encouragement, attempt to get him interested in the scent of the track to which you are pointing. Walk him the entire length of the track, if necessary. Should he want to move out on it, let him start to take the tracking line out. In any case of the dog's stopping his tracking in mid track, walk him the remaining distance. Insist that he always complete a track that he has started.

Problem: *The dog has the tendency to stay in the well-defined rows when tracking in a stubble field.*

Solution: This is a common type of behavior exhibited by most dogs when they first track in a stubble field. It is much easier for the dog to move through a stubble field if he keeps to these rows, just as it is easier for a person with exposed legs who attempts to walk through the field. The stubble can cut up a dog's legs and soft underbelly and should a person with bare legs pass through a stubble field that has a little height, they would come out with legs that show the visible penetration of these pieces of stubble. When the track cuts across the well-defined rows at an angle that almost parallels the track, the dog will tend to drift down a stubble row, probably following body odor that is also blown down these rows. A short distance later, the dog will head back to the track where he will start to follow and drift down another stubble row.

This is inexperience on the part of the dog, which can only

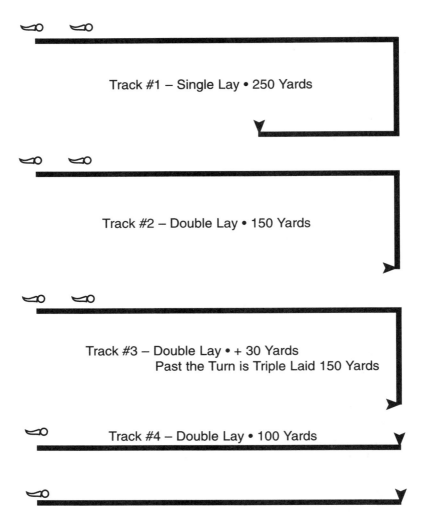

Track #1 – Single Lay • 250 Yards

Track #2 – Double Lay • 150 Yards

Track #3 – Double Lay • + 30 Yards
Past the Turn is Triple Laid 150 Yards

Track #4 – Double Lay • 100 Yards

**Track #5 – Double Lay • 100 Yards and Laid with the
Dog Ready to Start, Watching from the Stake.**

Procedure – The dog is to run the fifth track laid as soon as the Track
layer completes the track and by-passes the Handler.
Upon discovery of the article, the dog is praised and taken
to the start of Track #4, which he is to start on immediately.
Completing each track, the dog is to continue onto each track
in the reverse order in which they were laid.

Figure 31 • **Remotivation Tracks**

be cured by more work in stubble fields. The handler should be made aware of the track's exact location when angling across the stubble so that he can increase the tension on the line each time this drifting from the track is observed.

Problem: *The candidate for tracking is a young puppy that has no desire to retrieve at all. When a ball or glove is thrown, he ignores it and just wants to run around investigating everything but the thrown object. Since this dog is going to be used in obedience, shouldn't he be trained in obedience and to retrieve first before entering a tacking training program?*

Solution: The simple fact that the dog is a non-retriever has no bearing on his tracking ability and should not be a consideration of whether to train him in tracking or not. Teaching him to retrieve, whether by force or by inducement, will not put an instinct into him and has never been proven to be of any value in tracking training except that he would pick up and return the glove (sometimes) when he finds it. To obedience train the dog first will have no value when it comes to training him in tracking. It might have a detrimental effect, depending on how he is trained. If you want this dog to be a "Gung Ho" enthusiastic tracking dog, I would start his training immediately by resorting to food as the motivational force.

Problem: *The dog starting into tracking training is rather slow. During the first two weeks of tracking, he has never attempted to run the track, but rather works the track out at a normal walking pace. How do I speed up the dog?*

Solution: In all probability, you will never speed up the dog. If the dog entering tracking training is normally a quick type of dog, that is, he seems to do everything at a fast pace, then he'll always track at a fast pace, but if he is normally slow-paced, then he will, in all probability, remain slow-paced. Tracking training will not alter the natural characteristics of the dog.

Problem: *The dog has the tendency to start on a track well, but overshoots the turns badly with no apparent indication of loss of track. Once he is restarted, he will track each straight leg up to each turn with apparent ease. How do I get him to indicate loss of track sooner and to detect the track's new direction?*

Solution: Dogs that have been accelerated in their training during the third week when turns were first introduced usually exhibit this tendency. Handlers should never skip a day's schedule, even if they had to miss a day of training. Should a day be missed, always continue training by starting on the schedule with the day that was missed. If the dog hasn't skipped some days, then follow this procedure:

Continue to lay out the designed tracks that are called for in accordance with the schedule for the week you are in and continue the rate of advancement as specified. When the track layer makes a turn, he is to triple lay the first ten yards past the corner and place a food drop at the end of five paces past each turn. The food drops are to continue in this manner for a week of training. For the second week, the same distance is to be triple laid with the food drop placed at the end of the ten paces of triple laying. In the third week of training, the triple lay is still continued with the food drop being placed at the twenty pace mark. The fourth week of corrective training retains a food drop half way on the legs and the turns are to be single laid. After this week of utilizing the food drops, they are to be discontinued and normal tracking resumed.

Problem:: *The dog tracks well once started. The problem is that the dog doesn't start well at all. Once he is a distance past the first two stakes, he will begin to track poorly and with little zest and then picks up speed and performs well. Sometimes it will take ten minutes to get past the second marker flag.*

Solution: This is a common problem witnessed often at tracking tests and indicates lack of motivation to start. The dog

---

is usually not interested in the start and will wander about aimlessly with head up in the air, appearing more interested in things around him than he is in the possible presence of a track. In order to remotivate him, lay the tracks as follows:

The track layer should triple lay the start of the track to a point about ten paces past the second flag. A food drop midway between the two stakes, as well as at the end of the triple laid portion of the track, is to be instituted for about one week of tracking. At the end of this time, the triple lay is to be continued for another week, but the first food drop is discontinued. During the third week, the triple laid portion is dropped and the entire track is to be single laid with the second food drop to continue. At the end of this week of tracking, the food drop itself is discontinued.

Problem: *When following a track that enters high weed cover that is twice as tall as the dog and is difficult to maneuver through, the dog starts into the heavy cover, backs out, and looks as if he's lost the track. He will circle to cover all of the ground area up to the heavy cover, but will not enter it. This dog normally performs extremely well when there is no such heavy cover.*

Solution: Some dogs are reluctant to track through areas or even near areas that may represent a hostile environment to them. There could be several hundred reasons for their reluctance to enter such an area and it is really a waste of time to endeavor to theorize why. As long as it is possible to overcome this behavior with corrective training, we need not spend time attempting to fathom why. To overcome this behavior, we simply have to make the dog believe that this difficult area is short-lived and that within a few paces he'll be out of it. Tracks should be laid that will penetrate into the high weeded areas for just a few paces before coming back into shorter, more easily worked areas. The handler should move up beside the dog and really encourage the dog to enter at the point where the track layer entered. Once through a short distance of this type of cover, the dog will start to enter himself, but tentatively. Do not

---

increase the distance that he'll have to track in heavy cover until he is entering the short distance of heavy cover confidently. It is not necessary to have long tracks that incorporate the heavy cover, but rather short tracks of about 100 yards in length that have no turns. In this manner, you can have him run out several such tracks in one day and be over the problem within a week or two.

We had a Miniature Poodle that was almost ten years old entered in our tracking classes. It was almost blind and would freeze up as it approached a tree line. The shadows which the tree line cast seemed to cause the little dog a great deal of concern. By laying tracks that came closer and closer to these tree lines, we were finally able to convince the dog that it had nothing to fear. Although there were many occasions when the handler had to walk the dog past and through these tree lines with great encouragement. Within one year this little dog earned its Canadian and American tracking titles, along with its Canadian TDX title without ever having failed at a test. Shortly after completion of the TDX it was totally blind and still loved to track.

Problem: *The dog seems to track well and is still in the first weeks of training, but is losing interest by the time the third sequence of tracks are to be followed.*

Solution: Some dogs do not have the drive and interest that other dogs have when retrieving. This simply means that he is overworked and the number of tracks in each sequence has to be reduced. Drop the first track of each day and see if he can maintain interest in this load. Should it be necessary, drop the third sequence. If the dog is on one sequence, but three tracks per day, drop the first track designated in the training schedule for that week.

Problem: *When training a dog in TDX, the dog will go off the track where there are no tracks or crosstracks. When he is pulled to a stop, he seems to refuse the actual track and it takes quite a while to get him started again.*

Solution: This will occur often when training a dog in TDX, especially when the track is laid and then allowed to cool for a long period of time. What has probably happened is that someone, unknown to the handler or track layer, has crossed the track. In order to correct the situation, the track layer must let the handler know at the moment it appears if the dog is picking up another track that is not supposed to be there. The handler should only respond if the dog is about to commit himself to it. Calling the dog's name in an excited tone of voice, take several paces past that point while encouraging the dog to come and have a look at what the handler has found. Once past this point, the handler should come to a halt and command the dog to look for and follow the track he started on. At no time should the handler scold the dog for selecting another track to go with. The dog may be right if it does smell the same to him.

Problem: *When training a dog for TDX, the dog appears to lose interest in tracking, and it becomes more and more difficult to get him tracking again. His behavior seems to be one of "couldn't care less."*

Solution: This behavior exhibited by tracking dogs that are actively engaged in TDX training is the result of the increasing difficulty and hard work that the training demands. The dog should be taken off the training program for a few days and then placed on motivation tracks that are only 300 to 400 yards long, two to three turns, and only thirty minutes old. He will follow these tracks with ease and after a few days of such easy tracks, he can be put on the TDX program once more. Ensure that he gets a day's rest following a TDX type of track with a motivation track every day following this day of rest.

Problem: *The training schedule seems unduly demanding for the small breeds of dogs.*

Solution: Yes. It is. The training schedule as regards distances applies to the medium and large breeds of dogs and when a small breed, or toy, begins training, the handler should reduce

---

the advocated track sizes by 50% until the dog is performing well at the end of the sixth week. At this time, the handler should begin to lengthen the different legs until a total of 600 yards is reached.

Problem: *The dog seems to start well, but at some point he seems to lose interest, and no matter how long the handler waits, the dog doesn't resume the track.*

Solution: This usually indicates that the retrieve is not what he is doing. Many times I have found myself in this same position when I have attempted to base the training of a dog on his retrieving instinct when, in fact, the dog had been previously trained to retrieve. It does require more work on the handler's part to base his initial training on food, but this technique does keep the dog's interest and results in a trained tracking dog in an even shorter period of time.

It never fails to amuse me when I see the looks of disgust registering on the faces of new handlers when they discover that they are going to have to rely on food as a motivational force to train their dogs. Yet, they all swear by it when they end up receiving their Tracking Titles before the other dogs in the class.

The handler should never allow his dog to simply wander about when on a track. The track is continually aging while the dog is delaying. Should the dog appear to lose interest, the handler should quickly respond by going up to the dog, point to the ground where the track actually is and, while encouraging him to "find it," proceed in the direction of the track with the dog on a short lead.

Problem: *The dog is starting well, seems to track well, but on many occasions has indicated "loss of track" while in the middle of a straight leg where there is no change in vegetation.*

Solution: I have had to contend with this problem on several occasions and have no real answer as to why the dog should perform in this manner. It seems as if he wants to check out something that has passed over the track at that point, perhaps before the track had been laid. The handler usually follows for a distance and then realizes that it really isn't the real track that the dog is on. To counter this behavior, we have lengthened the tracking line so that the handler will track behind the dog at a specified distance, but still has extra line with which he can allow the dog to proceed further without the handler following. In this manner, the dog will indicate to the handler that it is a false trail before the handler has committed himself to following.

Problem: *The dog is slow to start, but seems to track very well once past the first turn. It seems as if he has no real interest in the track until that point and then really "turns on."*

Solution: The simplest way to overcome this problem with most dogs is to incorporate the "Starter Track" into his regular training program. This consists of the handler's leaving his dog on a *stay* command or restraining him while he lays a simple straight track of about 25 to 50 paces long a few minutes before putting the dog onto a regular track. Once laid, the handler runs his dog on the starter track, which the dog has seen him laying and then proceeding to run the regular track immediately after the dog has found the handler's article on the starter track. This starter track can also be used at a tracking test just before the dog is scheduled to track. Here the track can be laid right beside the road away from the field areas where the test is being conducted and out of sight of the other competing dogs.

Problem: *Occasionally the dog picks up articles that are not the articles that have been left on the track.*

Solution: Should a dog do this in training – PRAISE HIM – and then continue on the track. There is no way a handler can immediately determine whether or not that article may have some of the track layer's scent on it and if the dog has performed accurately, he must be praised. You'll obtain far better results by praising the dog for an occasional error than if you failed to praise him for a correct behavior.

Many times I have seen Tracking Dogs, even at Licensed Tests, pick up a coin, or a gum wrapper or something similar, that the track layer has inadvertently dropped while laying a track. One occasion in particular stands out since it involved my own dog in a demonstration for television.

A simulated incident involving a fleeing suspect was set up with a co-instructor playing the part of the suspect. During his flight, he was to lose his hat and bury his key case, which was supposed to be from a supposed stolen automobile. Near the end of the track my dog stopped, picked up something and brought it back to me. I discovered it was the identification tag bearing the license number of a car. Knowing that this was not part of the script, I put it in my pocket and continued on the track which we successfully completed. Imagine the surprise on my "suspect's" face when he discovered that he had accidentally dropped the tag, and that the dog had correctly identified it and retrieved it to me.

Problem: *My dog tracks very well, but he overshoots the turns very badly with no indication that he has even lost the track, yet once started on the track once more, he performs exceptionally well, until the next turn.*

Solution: Quite often you'll find a dog that is so interested in the track that his indication of "Loss of track" is so slight that the handler cannot read it with the result that the handler continues on behind the dog instead of reacting properly. This is no fault of the handler, but the indication given by the dog has to be intensified.

In order to make the dog more aware of the turn, we resort again to food. When the track layer lays the track, have him take a wiener with him. At the point where his turn is going to be, have him place the food on the ground and step on it. Then have him rub it on the ground before picking it up and continuing on to lay the next leg of the track. Ten paces from the turn have him leave a piece of the wiener directly on the track.

The dog will stop almost dead in his tracks once he comes

Tracking Dog Theory & Methods

across the smell of the food and when he picks out the new direction, he is immediately rewarded with an actual find of food. Praise is not required at this point, since the food is enough reward in itself. As time goes on, decrease the squashed food until he is identifying the turns and looking for the food drop that he knows is coming and, finally, discontinue the food drop itself.

Problem: *The dog doesn't seem to want to take starting scent at the starting stake and starts very badly between the starting flags.*

Solution: Another problem easily solved by the use of food. Have the track layer take a piece of wiener and deposit it on the ground at the start. He should then step on it and move the piece around the starting area, stepping on it again and again. When he starts laying the track, he should pick up the pieces so that none remain. At the fifteen pace mark, he should deposit one piece of the food and again at the 40 pace mark.

The dog will learn very quickly what awaits him when he starts and the smell of the ground-in food will get him interested in the start like never before. After a week of this, the ground-in food should cease, as well as the food drop at the fifteen pace mark, leaving the food drop remaining at the forty pace mark. Another week is required before this last drop is discontinued and periodically, about once every few weeks, it should be re-instituted on one track.

There is no field of dog training that is without problems, but in tracking training the number of problems seem to be few and are determined by the characteristics of the individual dog and the training he has received. In this chapter I have attempted to highlight those problems which seem commonplace in track and which I call "classic," since these seem to be the problems that most handlers run into. A rather simple rule which I follow seems to provide the answer to all of the tracking problems that I have encountered when training countless dogs to track.

---

1. If the dog is not giving the track his full attention when in training, then I am not providing the necessary motivation to keep him interested in the track. It is my fault.

2. If the dog is not learning the objective I have set for him to learn, I have designed the learning situation incorrectly for him to learn that objective. It is my fault.

3. If the dog cannot handle an unexpected situation, I have not prepared him for that situation. It is my fault.

To sum it all up in one sentence... *If the dog is not performing in the manner I expect him to perform, then I am doing something that has to be wrong.*
In scent work, the dog is the one that knows what he is doing and is always right while the handler, unable to determine just what or how he is doing it, can only set up the situation and hope that it will be conducive to the dog's learning if designed and implemented correctly.

Tracking
Trainers
Handbook

This chapter condenses all of the track designs, tracking schedules and includes a lesson format to be used by trainers conducting a tracking training program. Each lesson, starting with the first day and proceeding through the TD and TDX training is detailed with specific things the trainer should be looking for at each lesson. This section should be removed and taken into the field where the training is to be performed and the weekly assignments copied and handed out to the student as required. By studying each week's training as detailed in this book before going into the field for actual training, the instructor will be aware of procedures, possible problem areas and understand the short anecdotes appearing with each lesson. Should any problem appear to be developing during a lesson the book should be consulted immediately for corrective action.

Tracking Training Program
The tracking training program outlined in this precis is designed for use by anyone wanting to direct a tracking training program for novice and/or professional dog trainers. All of the

dogs should meet once each seven days in order for the instructor to determine if any problems are showing themselves and to provide designed situations conducive to the dog's learning how to use his/her nose to follow where another human being has walked, indicating any item that may have been dropped along the way. This precis covers the designed session from the introductory lesson through the weekly assignments necessary to provide a competent dog/handler tracking team.

Rules of Conduct

1. No scolding or chastisement whatever are permitted when tracking.

2. No obedience commands are to be enforced with the one exception of the "DOWN" when required in the program before starting the dog.

3. The tracking harness does not go on the dog at any other time except when the handler and dog are about to commence a track.

4. The track layer MUST map out all tracks more than 1 corner in size and must follow the handler approximately 60 feet behind.

5. All dogs must be watered immediately following a tracking session.

6. All tracks will run in a straight line on each leg. No track layer will curve his path to miss bushes, ditches, etc.

Due to the high temperatures found in most areas during the mid-day times, tracking sessions are best restricted to mornings or evenings, in order to make it as comfortable for the dog as possible.

Introduction to the Tracking Training Program

Equipment:
1. Non-restrictive tracking harness
2. Fifty foot light, weather proof tracking line
3. Six leather articles – different but hand size
4. Eight tracking stakes with observable flagging
5. Rain gear – coat, pants and boots
6. Drinking water from handler's locale and dish for dog
7. Mosquito repellent (for handler and dog)
8. Clipboard – pens – paper for map-making

Lesson 1
A. Lecture on necessity of each of the items mentioned under equipment.

B. Have each prospective handler lay a one corner track, deposit a small object smaller than a matchbook and return along same path and then find it.

C. Describe track laying – two reference points needed to walk in a straight line instead of in a curve.

D. Describe and demonstrate map marking of corners by using natural, observable changes in terrain, vegetation or natural markers at the exact point of direction change.

E. Describe importance of carrying extra article in case of overshoot.

Participation
1. Check retrieving instincts. Article thrown by (A) Handler (B) Instructor.

2. Start compulsive retrievers on first day schedule.

3. Start non-retrievers on same schedule using ten yard food drops.

Non-Retrievers: Finicky eaters to go on half rations earned only on track. Fussy eaters to receive 50% of normal volume on track and 50% at home. Chow Hounds to receive food drops as extra food on track.

Assign week's training chart–emphasize wind direction over the next week.

First Week Tracking Training Chart

Day	Track	Distance (Yds..)	Wind Direction	Lay
1	1	5	Into	D
	2	10	Into	D
	3	20	Into	D
2	1	10	Into	D
	2	20	Into	D
	3	40	Into	D
3	1	20	Into	D
	2	40	With	D
	3	80	With	D
4	1	40	With	D
	2	80	With	D
	3	160	With	D
5	1	80	With	D
	2	160	With	S
	3	320	With	S
6	1	160	With	S
	2	320	With	S
	3	400	With	S

D = Double laid track. The Track layer goes out and returns by the same route. The dog is started when the Track layer has returned.

S = Single laid track. The Track layer goes out, but does not return along the same route. The dog isn't started until the Track layer returns to the handler.

Lesson 2

1. Each dog to track instructor's track at the end (T4)

2. Into wind tracks
    A. 20 yds.. = T1
    B. 80 yds.. = T2
    C. 160 yds.. = T3

3. Instructor lays next track:
    A. 40 yds.. with the wind = T4

Observations:
   Watch for any peculiarities arising during all of these tracks, especially:

1. Motivational problems
2. Lead handling problems
3. When and where harness is put on
4. Allow dog to detect track as handler and dog approach.
5. Praise at climax and removal of harness.

Notes:

Second Week Tracking Training Chart

Day	Track	Distance (Yds..)	Wind Direction	Lay	Age
1	1	5	With	S	5 Min.
	2	10	With	S	5 Min.
	3	20	With	S	5 Min.
2	1	10	With	S	8 Min.
	2	20	With	S	8 Min.
	3	40	With	S	8 Min.
3	1	20	With	S	10 Min.
	2	40	With	S	10 Min.
	3	80	With	S	10 Min.
4	1	40	With	S	15 Min.
	2	80	With	S	15 Min.
	3	160	With	S	15 Min.
5	1	80	With	S	15 Min.
	2	160	With	S	15 Min.
	3	320	With	S	15 Min.
6	1	160	With	S	15 Min.
	2	320	With	S	15 Min.
	3	400	With	S	15 Min.

S = Single laid track, the Track layer goes out but does not return by the same route. The return route should be downwind at least 50 yards.

The dog is to be placed down, with his head even with the starting stake, over the trampled down square yard. Timing of track age commences with the track layers stepping out.

Lesson 3

1. Each handler to lay tracks for his partner and vice versa

2. All tracks with the wind

3. Final track to be laid by instructor (first corner)

4. Dog/handler team's tracking schedule to be reduced from 9 tracks per day to the 3 tracks per day as per the third wee training chart.
   a. Track No. 1 = 40 yds..
   b. Track No. 2 = 160 yds..
   c. Track No. 3 = 400 yds..
   d. Track No. 4 = 100 yds.. + 20 yds.. Triple lay into wind

Observations:
   Watch closely for:

1. Fringe following

2. Lead handling

3. Fringe following in crosswind of first leg

4. Trailing

5. Harness on – off and praising

6. Allow dog to detect track as approaching starting flag. If necessary, *down* dog with head beside starting flag. Wait several seconds, start dog. Handler doesn't move until dog is thirty feet away, moving in straight line on track.

7. Allow dog six feet each side of track, but with increased tension as dog moves off track.

Tracking Dog Theory & Methods

Track Design for the Third Week
Introduction of First Turn

Wind Direction

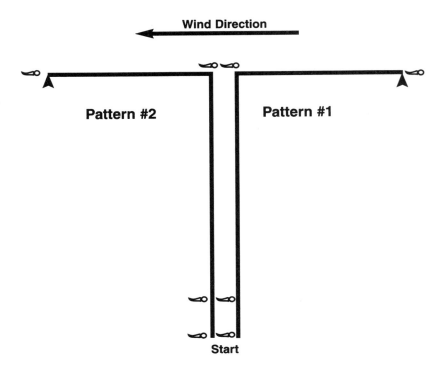

Pattern #2   Pattern #1

Start

Flags ⌐O

Article ▲

Corner Flags – Always placed on the side of the track, opposite the direction of the turn.

T – Triple Lay – The Track layer goes, returns and then goes out on the track again, meaning that he has passed over the same ground three different times.

Ss – Single Short Step Lay – The Track layer moves out on a single lay but moves his feet in a heel-to-toe fashion

S – Single Lay

Third Week Tracking Training Chart

Day	Track	First Leg (Yds..)	Second Leg (Yds..)	Wind	Lay	Age
1	1	100	20	Into	T	15 Min.
	2	100	40	Into	T	15 Min.
	3	100	80	Into	T	15 Min.
2	1	125	40	Into	Ss	15 Min.
	2	125	80	Into	Ss	15 Min.
	3	125	160	Into	Ss	15 Min.
3	1	140	80	Into	S	15 Min.
	2	160	160	Into	S	15 Min.
	3	200	200	Into	S	15 Min.
4	1	100	20	With	T	15 Min.
	2	100	40	With	T	15 Min.
	3	100	80	With	T	15 Min.
5	1	125	40	With	Ss	15 Min.
	2	125	80	With	Ss	15 Min.
	3	125	160	With	Ss	15 Min.
6	1	140	80	With	S	15 Min.
	2	160	160	With	S	15 Min.
	3	200	200	With	S	15 Min.

* Note – Follow Pattern #1 on Days 1, 2, 3
   Follow Pattern #2 on Days 4, 5, 6

Wind – Refers to the direction of the second leg with respect to the wind

T = Triple lay (Second leg only)

Ss = Toe to heel stepping on second leg only

S = Single lay throughout both legs

Lesson 4

1. Pull all stakes on final track laid by instructor and no corner stakes to be used from this time on.

2. Second stake at 30 yds..

3. Have handler see tracks being laid.

4. Keep number of tracks per team to three tracks per day after this session.

Track No. 1 Leg 1 = 100 yds.. + 150 yds..
Track No. 2 Leg 1 = 150 yds.. + 20 yds.. (last triple laid into wind)

Observation:
    Watch for:
        Lead Handling
        Starting Techniques
        Trailing or Fringe Following
        Tiring
        Guiding

Notes:

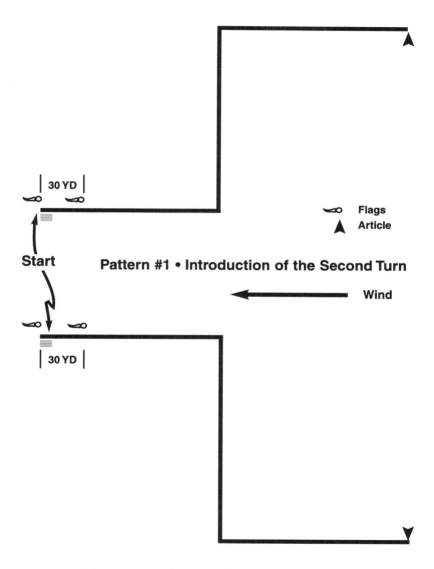

30 YD

Flags
Article

Start

Pattern #1 • Introduction of the Second Turn

Wind

30 YD

Pattern #1 • **Conclusion of the Second Turn**

Fourth Week Tracking Training Chart

Day	Track	Leg	Length(Yds..)	Wind	Lay	Age
1	1	1	100	Into	S	15 Min.
		2	75	cross	Sb	15 Min.
		3	25	Into	T	15 Min.
	2	1	100	Into	S	15 Min.
		2	100	cross	Sb	15 Min.
		3	50	Into	T	15 Min.
	3	1	125	Into	S	15 Min.
		2	125	cross	Sb	15 Min.
		3	100	Into	Ss	15 Min.
2	1	1	100	Into	S	15 Min.
		2	75	cross	Sb	15 Min.
		3	25	Into	Sb	15 Min.
	2	1	100	Into	S	15 Min.
		2	100	cross	Sb	15 Min.
		3	50	Into	Ss	15 Min.
	3	1	125	Into	S	15 Min.
		2	125	cross	Sb	15 Min.
		3	100	Into	Sb	15 Min.
3	1	1	100	Into	S	15 Min.
		2	75	cross	Sb	15 Min.
		3	25	Into	Sb	15 Min.
	2	1	100	Into	S	15 Min.
		2	100	cross	S	15 Min.
		3	50	Into	Sb	15 Min.
	3	1	125	Into	S	15 Min.
		2	125	cross	S	15 Min.
		3	100	Into	S	15 Min.

S = Single Lay

T = Triple Lay

Ss = Single Lay but toe-to-heel fashion

Sb = Single Lay but the first 10 paces are
   only heel-to-toe fashion

Note – First Three Days Use Pattern #1
   Second Three Days Use Pattern #2

Lesson 5

1. Second stake at thirty yards

2. Handler does not see track being laid, but sees map prior to starting track.

3. One track – laid by other handler – not a partner

4. Third corner is to be an acute angle laid so that the leg leading to the acute angle runs with the wind.

5. Allow the dog to work out the corners.

6. Acute Angle: Have handler encourage dog to swing around him by slowly revolving clockwise.

Observation:
Watch for correct angle on the acute turn.

Watch for handler tendency to one step himself off the track or corner.

Let dog work it out.

Notes:

The Third Turn

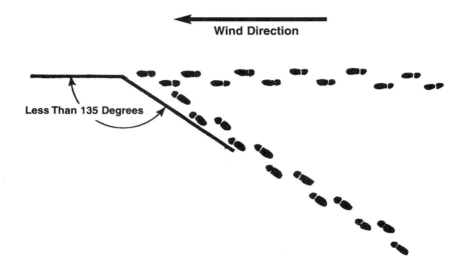

Wind Direction

Less Than 135 Degrees

Laying the Acute Angle Properly

Fifth Week Tracking Training Chart

Day	Track	Leg 1	Leg 2	Leg 3	Leg 4	Age of Track
1	1	100	75	100	50	15 Min.
2	1	100	100	125	75	15 Min.
3	1	100	100	125	100	20 Min.
4	1	100	100	100	150	20 Min.
5	1	125	125	125	125	25 Min.
6	1	100	100	150	150	25 Min.

* Note – The Last Corner Should be the Acute Angle and the Handler Should be Made Aware of the Track's Map, Prior to Starting.

No Stakes are to Mark Corners, nor the Article's Position.

Position of the Handler a few yards past turn

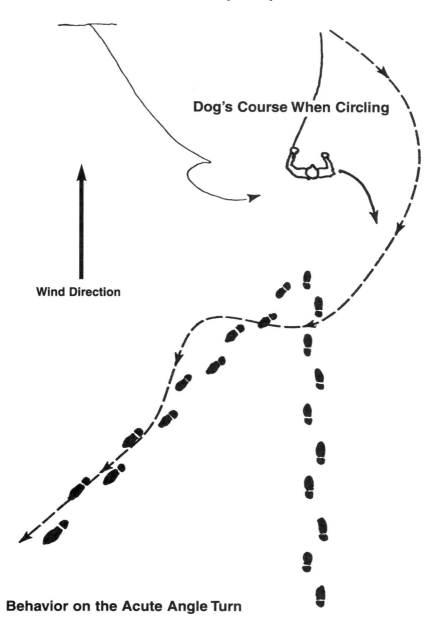

Dog's Course When Circling

Wind Direction

Behavior on the Acute Angle Turn

Lesson 6

1. Instructor to lay a test track for each handler and triple lay the track.

2. Allow the handler no opportunity to see the track being laid nor the completed map.

3. Have the handler put his dog on track at 15 – 25 minutes

4. Handler is to be left on his own while everyone else does their track the same.

5. Each handler is to return to instructor after locating the article at which time he must draw a map of the track showing all corners and the direction of each leg.

Notes:

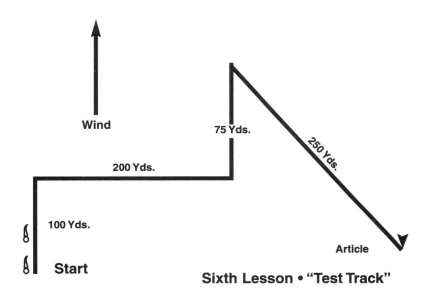

Wind

75 Yds.

200 Yds.

250 Yds.

100 Yds.

Article

Start

Sixth Lesson • "Test Track"

Sixth Week Tracking Training Chart

Day	Track	Length	Corners	Corner Content	Track
1	1	4-500	4	1A-1B-2R	25 Min.
2	1	4-500	4	1A-1B-2R	25 Min.
3	1	4-500	4	1A-1B-2R	25 Min.
4	1	4-500	4	1A-1B-2R	25 Min.
5	1	4-500	4	1A-1B-2R	25 Min.
6	1	4-500	4	1A-1B-2R	25 Min.

* NOTE:
1. Handler must keep a constant pressure on the tracking line.
2. Handler must stop moving when the dog exhibits doubt.
3. Handler must "observe" on and off track signs.
4. The line is never to touch the ground, even on circling.

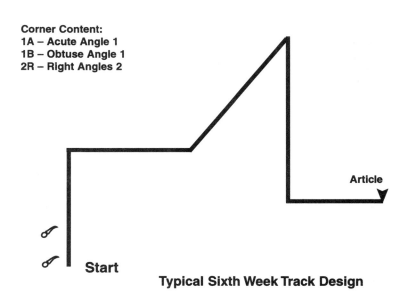

Corner Content:
1A – Acute Angle 1
1B – Obtuse Angle 1
2R – Right Angles 2

Article

Start

Typical Sixth Week Track Design

Example Chart

Wind	Temp.	Humidity	Veg.	Weather	Time	Score	Factor	Hump
Low	Low	High	Lush	Overcast	Morn.			
3	3	3	3	3	3	18	X5	90 m
High	Hot	Low	None	Bright	Mid			
1	1	1	1	1	1	6	X5	30 m

Determining the Hump

Wind	Temp.	Humidity	Veg.	Weather	Time	Score	Factor	Hump
Low	Low	High	Lush	Overcast	Morn.	3	5	
Med.	Med.	Med.	Dry	Cloud	Aft.	2	5	
High	Hot	Low	None	Bright	Mid.	1	5	

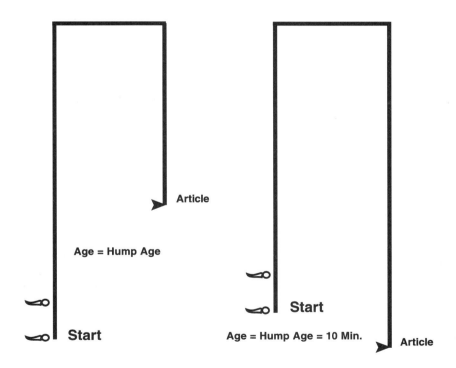

Article

Age = Hump Age

Start

Start

Age = Hump Age = 10 Min.

Article

Track Design to Approach Hump

Seventh Week Tracking Training Chart

Track	Track	Length(YDS..)	Turns	Age
1	1	500	3	25 Min.
2	1	500	3	30 Min.
3	1	500	3	35 Min.
4	1	500	3	40 Min.
5	1	500	3	45 Min.
6	1	500	3	50 Min.

*Note – Should the dog suddenly stop tracking at point
Along the track, during this week, encourage him and walk
him on a short lead throughout the track. If He starts to
move out on his own, give him more line and quietly
follow him.*

Lesson 8
Reading the Dog
1. Track layer to lay track and have persons follow alongside
twenty paces from the actual track.

2. At the turns, before the turn is made, one of the persons is
dropped off with instructions to wait and record the behavior of
one assigned portion of dog's anatomy for LOSS and DISCOV-
ERY of track.

3. Continue to complete track in this manner.

4. Instructor to record all observable behavior as he follows
team on track and pick up each person as turns are made.

5. Person to continue recording behavior of selected portion of
anatomy as tracking continues.

6. At the end, instructor collects data and determines most reliable and observable behaviors and informs handler.

	Loss		Find
Head			
Tail			
Course			
Body			
Pace			
Other			

Week 9 Schedule

Track	Track	Length (YDS..)	Turns	Age
1	1	4 – 600	3	30 Min.
2	1	4 – 600	3	45 Min.
3	1	4 – 600	4	60 Min.
4	1	4 – 600	4	75 Min.
5	1	4 – 600	4	90 Min.
6	1	4 – 600	4	105 Min.

Week 10 Schedule

Track	Track	Length (YDS..)	Turns	Age
1	1	5 – 700	4	45 Min.
2	1	5 – 700	4	1 Hr.
3	1	5 – 700	4	1hr. 15 Min.
4	1	5 – 700	4	1hr. 30 Min.
5	1	5 – 700	4	1hr. 45 Min.
6	1	5 – 700	4	2 Hrs.

Conclusion of Week 10 – Certification

The "Non–Retriever"

1. The dog must go onto half his regular daily rations and that half he does get, he must earn on the track.

2. Use some NOURISHING food that the dog really loves.

3. Proportion his "half ration" prior to each training session.

4. Follow the food drop schedule listed below.

Day	Distance of food drop from the previous food group								
	No.1	No.2	No.3	No.4	No.5	No.6	No.7	No.8	No. 9
1	10	10	10	10	10	10	10	10	10
2	10	10	10	10	10	10	10	10	10
3	10	15	20	25	30	35	40	45	50
4	10	15	20	25	30	35	40	45	50
5	15	25	35	45	55	65	75	85	95
6	25	35	45	55	65	75	85	95	100
8	35	45	55	65	75	85	95	100	100
9	35	45	55	65	75	85	95	100	100
10	35	45	55	65	75	85	95	100	100
11	35	45	55	65	75	85	95	100	100
12	35	45	55	65	75	85	95	100	100
13	35	45	55	65	75	85	95	100	100
14	35	45	55	65	75	85	95	100	100

Once corners have commenced, have 1 food drop in the half leg.
Third lesson: Stuff glove with food.
Fourth Lesson: Reward with food after discovery of glove.
Normal feed resumes after two weeks.

Stamina Increase

Day	Track Length (YDS..)	# of Corners	Track Age
1	800 yds..	3	1 Hr.
2	1600 yds..	6	1 Hr.
3	2000 yds..	8	1 Hr.
4	3000 yds..	12	1 Hr.
5	3000 yds..	12	1.5 Hr.

1. Number of Article – 1
2. Terrain – Varying types of Vegetation

T.D.X. Tracking Program

Lesson 1 – *Starts*

Track Criteria
A. Number of tracks – 4, 1 hour old
B. Tracks all straight – 100 yards each
C. Dog and handler 90° to track's direction
D. Only one stake at start
E. One square yard trampled by stake
F. One article on each track

Observations:
1. Handler not to guide, step or in any way indicate track's direction.

2. Handler not to follow until dog has positively identified track's direction and has moved out to end of line.

3. Tracks to be run one after another.

Tracking Dog Theory & Methods

Week 12
Tracking Schedule – 3 Tracks Per Week

Track #1   Length   –   1500 yds..
            Corners   –   6
            Articles   –   1
            Age   –   1.5 Hr.

Track #2   Length   –   400 yds..
            Corners   –   3
            Articles   –   1
            Age   –   30 Min.

Track #3   Length   –   1500 yds..
            Corners   –   6
            Articles   –   1
            Age   –   2 Hr.

Special Techniques

1. Always start dog at right angles to track.

2. Wait until dog is moving out in a straight line and has reached the end of the line before following.

Lesson 2 – *Restarts*

Track Criteria
A. Number of Tracks – 1
B. Turns – 4
C. Length – 500 yds..
D. Age – 30 minutes
E. Articles – 6

Observations:
1. Handler to drop to one knee and coax dog to retrieve.

2. Handler to place glove out of dog's sight.

3. Handler to allow a few moments of praise and let dog settle down.

4. Handler to start dog without moving position until dog has reached site of article and is tracking out once more.

Tracking Schedule – Week 13

Track #1	Length	–	1500 yds..
	Corners	–	6 – 8
	Articles	–	6
	Age	–	2 Hrs. 15 Min.
Track #2	Length	–	400 yds..
	Corners	–	3
	Articles	–	1
	Age	–	30 Min.
Track #3	Length	–	1500 yds..
	Corners	–	6-8
	Articles	–	6
	Age	–	2 Hrs. 30 Min.

Special Techniques
1. On days of rest, run the restart track design shown in Lesson 2.

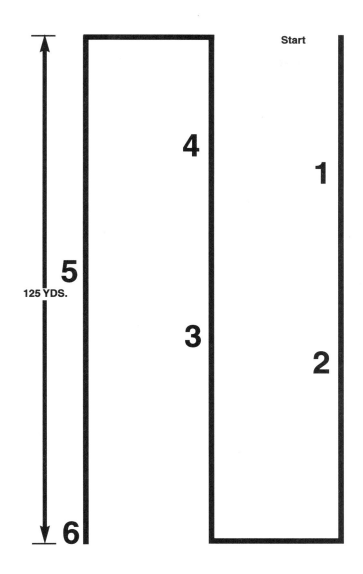

125 YDS.

Start

Restart Track Design

Lesson 3 – Roads

Track Criteria
A. Four separate tracks
B. Each track to be 100 yds.. long
C. Each track to be bisected by a road of 20 – 40 ft.
D. Each track age to be about 1 ht. old
E. Each track to be terminated with one article

Handling Techniques
1. When the dog reaches the road and IF he appears bewildered at the sudden track's end, encourage him to cross the road.

2. All tracks to be performed on in succession by each dog.

3. The handler must not completely cross the road, but must allow the dog enough lead length to reach the other side when casting.

Observation:
1. Roads are simply obstacles. When the handler reaches one and the dog cannot pick up a new direction – have him cross it and try.

Week 14
Tracking Schedule – 3 Tracks Per Week

Track #1	Length	–	1500 yds..
	Corners	–	6 – 8
	Articles	–	6
	Age	–	2 Hrs. 45 Min.
	Roads	–	1 Narrow Paved Road
Track #2	Length	–	400 yds..
	Corners	–	3
	Articles	–	1
	Age	–	30 Min.
	Roads	–	None
Track #3	Length	–	1500 yds..
	Corners	–	6-8
	Articles	–	6
	Age	–	3 Hr.
	Roads	–	1 Wide Paved Road

Special Techniques
1. Handler to run up on line as dog approaches road, then decrease tension as dog reaches road and cross road behind dog as dog does.

Tracking Dog Theory & Methods

Lesson 4 – Crosstrack Training
Track Criteria
A. One track as per "crosstrack training design"

B. Crosstrack as per design

C. Crosstrack laid by second party 30 minutes after track has been started.

D. Dog started on track 1 hour after it was laid. (Timing starts when track laying began.)

E. Substantial weight difference between track layer and crosstrack layer.

Observations:
1. Handler to allow dog to investigate any crosstrack he wants to — NO SCOLDING.

2. If dog commits on crosstrack, the handler is to break dog's attention through excited actions and verbal enticement while continuing on a few paces past crosstrack.

3. Once past crosstrack, encourage dog to start tracking again.

Tracking Schedule – Week 15
Every Day as Per Design

Day	Crosstrack Laid At:	Dog Start	Track Age	Crosstrack Age	Differential in Scent Strength
1	30 Min.	1 Hr.	1 Hr.	30 Min.	30 Min.
2	45 Min.	90 Min.	90 Min.	45 Min.	45 Min.
3	60 Min.	2 Hr.	2 Hr.	60 Min.	60 Min.
4	60 Min.	2¼ hr.	135 Min.	75 Min.	75 Min.
5	75 Min.	2½ Hr.	2½ Hr.	75 Min.	75 Min.
6	90 Min.	3 Hr.	3 Hr.	90 Min.	90 Min.

Special Techniques
1. No scolding when committed to crosstrack.
2. Substantial weight difference between track layer and crosstrack layer.

Tracking Dog Theory & Methods

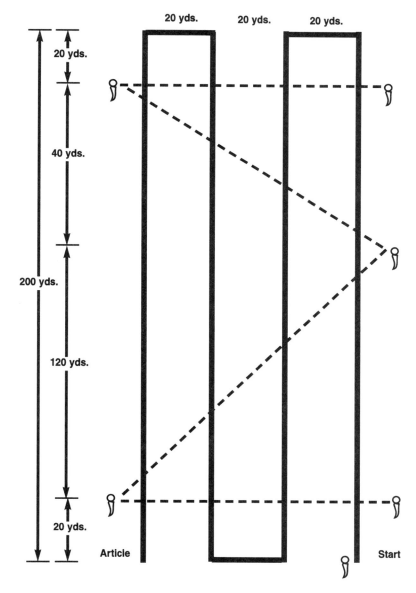

20 yds. **20 yds.** **20 yds.**

20 yds.

40 yds.

200 yds.

120 yds.

20 yds.

Article

Start

Crosstrack Training Design

Lesson 5 – Starter Track

Track Criteria
A. Track layer lays starter track as per design.
B. Track layer lays full TDX track.

1. Length — 1500 yds..
2. Corners — 6 – 8
3. Articles — 3
4. Roads — 1
5. Age — 3 hrs.

C. Crosstracks on starter track and TDX track laid one hour after each track has been completed.

D. Crosstracks on TDX track widely spaced.

E. Crosstracks on "starter track" per design

F. Three hours after "starter track" laid dog is to be put on starter track and then the TDX track.

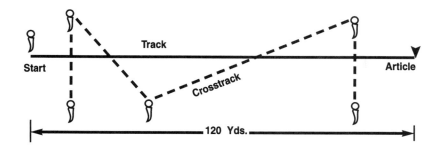

TDX (Crosstrack) Starter Track

Track #1A Starter Track
    1B TDX Track
        Age – 3 Hrs. 15 Min.

Track #2 Length   –   400 yds..
        Corners   –   3
        Articles –   1
        Age   –   30 Min.

Track #3A Starter Track
    3B TDX Track
        Age 3 1/2 Hours

Special Techniques
    Ensure track passes through varied vegetation, underbrush, across drainage ditches, through trees and crosses a paved road.

Lesson 6 — Step tracking

Track Criteria
A. Lay full TDX track.
B. Cross a corner of a plowed field, hard clay or sand twice.
C. First time — Several paces
    Second time — 30 – 40 paces
D. Ensure track possesses different difficulties, such as brush, fence lines, etc.

Track Criteria

- A. Length   –   1500 – 2000 yds..
- B. Corners   —   6 – 9
- C. Articles   —   3
- D. Age   —   3 hrs. +
- E. Roads   —   1 – 2
- F. Crosstracks   —   2 – 3

* Note 1. Always rest dog one day.
         2. Second track = Motivational track
         3. Rest dog one day.
         4. TDX Track

Enter TDX Test and Obtain Title.

Notes

Notes

Notes

Notes